THE CELL

A Story of Tragedy and Survival

by Barry Beck

 FriesenPress

One Printers Way
Altona, MB R0G 0B0
Canada

www.friesenpress.com

Copyright © 2024 by Barry Beck
First Edition — 2024

This Book has been designed using assets from Freepik.com

All rights reserved.

No part of this publication may be reproduced in any form, or by any means, electronic or mechanical, including photocopying, recording, or any information browsing, storage, or retrieval system, without permission in writing from FriesenPress.

ISBN
978-1-03-830534-3 (Hardcover)
978-1-03-830533-6 (Paperback)
978-1-03-830535-0 (eBook)

1. BIOGRAPHY & AUTOBIOGRAPHY, PERSONAL MEMOIRS

Distributed to the trade by The Ingram Book Company

Table of Contents

Author's Note   ix
Foreword   xi
Foreword   xii
Introduction   xiv

Sleepless in Pennsylvania   3
Elvis Has Left the Building   9
Creed   13
When the Redbird Sings   15
Sonny and The King   19
Knockout   23
Don't Cry For Me   27
Pepe Comes to Broadway   31
"Father Time"   35
Northlands Adrenaline   37
Big Bo   43
Pav Comes to The Big Apple   47
Bone Crackling   55
Ted, Pav and Rexi   59
Mark   67
The Dream   71
Court and More Court   77

Brock Cameron Beck	79
Back to Osoyoos, B.C.	83
Danny The Kid	87
Hong Kong, Here We Come	89
Summertime Blues	93
The Call	95
No One Here	99
Hamilton Crime Unit	103
Prison Cell	113
The Tornado	119
Vancouver Memorial	121
Osoyoos Bound	125
Copper Cove	131
Hong Kong S.A.R.	135
The Wanna-Be Gangsta!	139
Jaskiran Grewal: Inside Help	143
To Plead or Not to Plead	147
An American Hero	149
Wanna-Be Gangsters	151
Serendipity	159
Dedication	*164*

Barry & Brock

Barry Beck

Mark Pavelich

Author's Note

It was exhausting to write this book. I hope it will help people through trauma. My son's murder gave me an opportunity that I never would have had. I committed to that opportunity to write, to better myself and help others. I understand the commitment phase. The commitment is the healer for me. Destiny's path can be a difficult one. It can be a great opportunity to find inner strength you thought you never had.

Barry Beck
Professional hockey player

Foreword

"Leader" is the first word that comes to mind when defining the character of Barry Beck. From the moment my father pointed Barry Beck out in his junior days, saying, "Watch Barry Beck: now *that's* a hockey player," to watching him captain the New York Rangers, I was always excited to see him play.

The pages of this book tell the pure truth of a man who has achieved worldly success—not just as a hockey player, but as a humanitarian in the arena of mental health.

Barry's story dives deep into his personal traumas—two major life events that took him by storm: losing his son, Brock, to murder, and his dear friend, Mark Pavelich, to suicide. Any person who has been through any kind of adversity can connect to, learn from and grow through this book. Barry doesn't hold anything back.

I'm honored to call Barry my friend, and I encourage anyone who reads this masterpiece to pay close attention. It will help ignite your own personal healing.

Ryan Phillips
Author
2X TEDx speaker
Global mental health advocate TV & film Producer (True Redemption)

Foreword

Our lives are a collection of stories.

In each self-introduction and conversation, we are continuously constructing and reconstructing narratives of who we are and who we wish to be.

Telling stories comes naturally to us, and because of this, we often take for granted our roles as authors. We often forget to give ourselves credit for the ways that we seamlessly interweave events into the storylines of our lives.

And it often takes an unexpected – and sometimes unwelcome – interruption to realize our active authorship role. In the physical act of writing (the traditional pen and paper way), these unexpected events may be a severe case of writer's block or running out of ink. In the living of life, these interruptions come in the form of surprising events that disrupt the previous flow of our lives – new relationships, moving to a new home, the loss of a loved one. When confronting these events, we may find ourselves frozen with the pen in our hands, wondering to ourselves, *what do I do with this information? Where does it fit in my storyline? Where do I even begin?*

In *"The Cell,"* Barry Beck invites us to bear witness to his story. He narrates the ups and downs of his career as a professional ice hockey player – forming and fragmenting relationships, hurting and healing from injury, finding and leaving places he has called home. Although he is no stranger to adversity, Barry finds himself grappling to make sense of perhaps the most painful experience a parent can endure: the murder of their child.

In the wake of the murder of his son, Brock, Barry does not pretend to have the answers to overcoming grief. He describes finding himself in the dark, dense space of his "cell" of heartache, not knowing how to seek help nor how to help himself. We stand together with him as he grasps the pen in his hand, wondering how his story will continue.

Foreword

But just as hurting is not linear, neither is healing. Throughout his narrations of light and dark, Barry's voice is honest and heartfelt. He boldly peers through every crack of his breaking heart, but in doing so, shows us precisely where hope shines through.

To engage with this book is not only to bear witness to a remarkable process of storying, but of re-storying. In the face of one of the most painful experiences imaginable and despite being struck with the most unexpected of occurrences, Barry picks up the pen and chooses to keep writing. To not only make sense of what has happened, but to make *new meaning* from it. In establishing the Brock and Mark Scholarship Fund, which supports secondary students in Hong Kong to pursue studies in mental health-related fields, and in founding *FallinStars,* a mental health awareness-raising initiative, Barry transforms potent experiences of pain into brilliant beacons of hope and opportunity.

Ultimately, Barry's story is a deep dive into the human experience. Of riding the dynamic waves of life. Of hurting. Of hurting so much that we don't know how to *begin* healing, or whether it is even possible to heal. Of sticking it out long enough to discover that progress in healing *is* possible even when it feels slow at times. To kindle a flame of hope from what feels like nothing at all. To watch that flame grow into a fire. And finally, to realize that flickers of hope burn within us, even when we don't always notice them.

Stephanie Ng
Founder & Executive Director, Body Banter
Mental Health Advocate

Introduction

As a multiple trauma survivor, mental health advocate and author of *Motocross Saved My Life From Its Darkness*, it is a great honor to oblige my friend Barry Beck's request to provide the foreword for his highly anticipated memoir. Beck, of National Hockey League fame, grew up about an hour's drive from me, but I never met him personally until the day my daughter was born in 1994. By this time, even though we had traveled to rinks often to watch him play, his playing days were behind him. A successful career? An enigmatic career cut short, due to many injuries and circumstances out of his control?  However you look at it, Barry Beck will go down in my mind, as one of the most feared, and greatest defensemen of all in the National Hockey League.

I will also never forget the impression Barry left on me that first time we did meet. As a former professional Motocross racer, I had broken my right leg five times, and had numerous other broken bones before my life-changing spinal cord injury in 2011. I had gotten used to being beat down physically, but always knew what I had to do to rebound. My rituals soon included physical, mental and emotional escape from realities that I had grown tired of. I always liked a good adrenaline rush, and where I would meet Barry on this late August day, I found no shortage there.

It is not my place to tell Barry's story, or what we were up to on this particular day. I am grateful that Barry's kindness and sincerity in honor of my daughter's birth had such a profound impact on me. Barry, for the most part, is soft-spoken, and I felt compelled to reach out to him after the immeasurable loss of his son. I had also followed along with paramount concern for my old friend when Mark Pavelich died. I believe that Barry did what any loving brother or father would do in an unthinkable situation. Barry Beck and his teammates at Fallin Stars and Brock and Mark are all channeling their inner Hero and will never give up.

Introduction

Barry Beck is competitive, sports-minded, musically inclined and an articulate writer. Based on the life experiences that he has lived, coupled with his current mental health resolve, I too am extremely excited to read his brave and courageous life account. Thank you for allowing me to share my journey with you Barry. I am proud of you for your commitment and for not giving up on yours.

Getting a book to print, and sharing your story, Barry, is amazing.

Congratulations! We all have a story. You encouraged me when I was down. You reminded me that it was okay, as long as we learned to love, and when we struggled, we struggled as well as we could.

From Vancouver's Eastside, to hockey stardom, the injuries, the love of the game, the personal tragedies, coupled with his commitment to solidify lasting legacies for his late son Brock Beck, and good friend Mark Pavelich, while continuing to advocate for people by normalizing mental health conversations and initiatives, Barry Beck's story is a must read!

Brent 'Airmail' Worrall
Author I Motocross Saved My Life From Its Darkness
www.brentworrall.com

THE CELL

Sleepless in Pennsylvania

September, 2022

The 15-hour flight from Hong Kong seemed routine now, as I'd done it many times, and business class is the only way I can do overseas flights as I'm just too big for economy and run the risk of cramping.

On overseas flights, I have to make sure that I include all my meds from my angioplasty procedure – plus sleeping pills that I used regularly since the murder of my son.

Being consumed with hate, anger and resentment eats away at you over time and drains you of all energy. It also dishonors both Brock's and Mark legacy, at a time when my sole purpose in life had become building their legacies and forgetting about my own.

This is where my sleeping pill usage had brought me. Forgetting about myself and starting to isolate more and more.

After my son's murder and the subsequent suicide of Mark, I never had the chance to grieve as I was trying to look after everyone else. The trap had been set and I fell into it. Hard.

On the flight, I had to make sure that I brought enough sleeping pills with me to last the trip. In Hong Kong, I don't need a prescription; I can go directly to the pharmacy and get any pill I desire. This cuts out the middleman (doctor) and saves money just like an addict. That's what I'd become – a pill-popping addict who now needed the sleeping pills just to function, not to sleep.

In Hong Kong it's called zopiclone but in the USA it's known as ambien.

My body's tolerance to the pills had become overwhelming. I was now taking 60 - 75 pills within a 24-hour period. This amount put me into the critical phase and was endangering my life. I tried to hide it, but my close friends knew what was going on because of my isolation. It wasn't who I am, but rather what I had become.

||| THE CELL |||

I had tried to wean myself off the pills over a two-year period but was unsuccessful. I would go a week without sleeping and that's all I could last before having to take the pills again to get some sort of rest.

I didn't even remember the sleep, as the pills would just knock me out – no dreams – and they wouldn't even work all the time.

I was now taking 15 pills (10 mg each) starting at 11:30 at night. Maybe I got two hours of sleep, depending on my state of mind. If I didn't sleep, I'd take 15 more. That's 30. If you have revenge on your mind constantly, you will not sleep no matter how many pills you take. There are no excuses, just the reality of what I'd become.

I would take 15 more pills at 9:00 in the morning and 15 more for my afternoon power nap. I didn't even remember if I was sleeping. Maybe I threw in another 15 because it had become the only way to get any rest. That was 75 pills over a 24-hour period that I was doing for six months before I was asked to come to New York — insanity at its peak!

I had to be careful going through customs, as I knew I needed a prescription. In Hong Kong, sleeping pills are categorized at the same level with heroin and cocaine. It didn't make any sense to me, but I had no one to blame except myself. I had trouble being kind to myself because I was now an addict.

I had been through withdrawals once and had to call an ambulance to my residence. The sweating, cramping and the tremors had put me over the edge. I wouldn't wish it upon my worst enemy. When I arrived at the hospital, the doctor thought I was having a heart attack until I notified him how many sleeping pills I was taking. Then he knew I was going through withdrawals.

When I was in New York, the PowerPoint presentation for the Rangers Alumni went well. The Rangers' front office had been good to me. Even though I was critical of them over the way they handled Mark Pavelich's suicide, or the way they *didn't* handle it, I always thought they were a first-class organization. If you're going to be a good pro, you have to be consistent; that goes for pro teams as well.

A couple of days after the PowerPoint, I was to attend the golf tournament and dinner. The only problem was, I was running out of pills. Twice I had used them and they didn't work. I had counted before I left Hong Kong and thought I had enough. I was now in dangerous territory.

The golf tournament was at the Westchester Country Club, outside of New York City. It had been about 35 years since the last one I had attended. I had found out that the Rangers' doctor would be attending and thought I could possibly get a prescription from him for my pills. I would need them for my flight back. My window for using them was now down to every six hours. If not then the withdrawals would kick in and it was happening at the dinner. As I've said, I needed the pills now just to function.

When I found the doctor and told him how many pills I was using, he was beside himself. He couldn't believe it.

"How many pills are you using," he asked. "60-75 every 24 hours." I replied.

"That's enough to kill any normal human being," he said. "I can't give you a prescription in time, plus I wouldn't do it as I would be risking my license — but, more importantly, your life. You need help!"

As those words resonated, my withdrawals kicked in. The doctor was good friends with Glen Sather, who I was now talking with. He knew there was something wrong. I now had severe stomach cramps — not the kind you get from food poisoning but like a hamstring muscle cramp. When they're in your stomach, there is nothing you can do except endure them. I have a high tolerance for physical pain, but the withdrawals knocked me off my feet. It was embarrassing to say the least. I travelled all this way to have it unfold before my very eyes. Just horrible and embarrassing.

I waited outside trying to regroup but the sweat was pouring out of me and I could not get comfortable. As I waited, Glen Sather came out and said he would give me a ride back to the city. We talked a little on the way back, but it was difficult for me to even breathe. My neck was starting to swell, and all these complications were setting in.

Before I knew it, we were back at the hotel. I began to open the door when Glen said, "Barry I'd like to talk with you." I immediately knew this was like an intervention. I had five pills upstairs in my room, and although they wouldn't make me sleep, at least I might feel better for an hour.

Glen told me, "We want to offer you our help. I don't care if I have to pay for it myself. All you have to do is say yes and we'll start the process right now."

By no means was I ready, but you never are with an intervention. I now started to negotiate my ass off, as I knew it was over.

"Can I have until 6:00 am, please?" It was now 9:30 pm.

"You have 20 minutes to pack. Then a car will pick you up and take you to the New York Presbyterian Hospital where you will detox and be evaluated."

I was crushed. There was no way around it. It was time to get the help I needed, and I knew it. I thanked Glen and went upstairs to pack.

The withdrawals kept coming as I came back downstairs after packing. The ride from the west side to the east seemed to take forever. This was all last-minute, so I don't think anyone was prepared.

The Rangers were now in contact with the NHL Alumni Association, whose social worker is Jerry Jormakka. I had talked with Jerry a number of times after Mark's suicide and respected him a lot for being the only social worker with the Alumni. One social worker for an entire organization is not nearly enough as far as I was concerned, but I was in no position to be critical now.

⦀ THE CELL ⦀

Upon my arrival at the hospital, part of my evaluation involved being taken to the psych ward. I didn't agree with this at all. I was put into a small room, without any contact with anyone for seven hours. There were four big security guards protecting the ward, so there was no escaping. It was never quiet. I was getting more and more pissed off. Nobody to blame except me, I thought. You do the crime, now do the time. The crime didn't justify me being in the psych ward, but it is what it is. Pay the piper.

After my evaluation, I was moved to a semi-private room and then a private one. I was put on medication to help with my cramping. I had a lot of time to think. At the golf tournament, Ron Greschner, Tom Laidlaw and Dave Maloney were all there for me. Being former teammates, that meant a lot. Ron Greschner and I go way back, as Ron and my brother Murray played junior hockey together for Ernie McIean and the New Westminister Bruins — for whom I would eventually play three years of junior hockey.

There was also Adam Graves. Adam and my good friend, Rob Ingraham, were close. Adam had given me a big hug when I left the tournament on the way back to the city.

You will not meet any more supportive teammates than this group, and I thought of that while in the hospital. The support and love I felt kept me going.

It's what you think about when you have to surrender and that's what I had to do. Surrendering is not in my blood. It goes against everything I was taught growing up in East Vancouver. On the street there is no surrendering.

I had texted Jerry Jormakka and let him know about the psych ward episode and he apologized. He told me that they wanted to move me to a treatment facility in Pennsylvania called Brookdale that was located in the Pocono mountains. My five-day trip was now going to be extended.

After two days at New York Presbyterian, a car was going to take me on the two-hour drive to the Poconos. My driver would be the start of getting to know the Brookdale staff, most being recovering addicts, alcoholics or both.

When I arrived at Brookdale I was literally stripped of everything. Your possessions are taken and checked for alcohol or drugs. Your clothes are removed and you're asked to bend over and cough as two workers check your anal cavity for any contraband. It's degrading but necessary. Any possessions that have alcohol, such as deodorant, cologne or sanitizer are confiscated. You're given green scrubs to wear as you begin your detox. There are three colored liners: Red, yellow and blue. Red is strictly detox. Amber is a little more freedom, while blue you can move about the grounds freely. There are many cameras, well over 100, with tight security. They keep the men and women separated, as rehab romance can happen quickly.

You have a structured schedule, starting with wakeup at 6:00 am, but you are awakened throughout the night. The techs will do room checks unannounced at any given time. You have a curfew. You may be given a warning for breaking the rules, depending on what it is, but do it twice and you will be asked to leave.

The first couple of days I just stayed to myself and took everything in. I was still shaky but with regular doctor's appointments began to feel better. I learned a long time ago that rookies are made to be seen and not heard, so that's what I did. I'd been a leader most of my life but over the past six months my addiction had turned me into a follower — something that disgusted me.

I had 30 days to build my foundation of education on addiction. It doesn't happen overnight. For me this was all about sorting out my emotions. My guilt, anger, resentment and acceptance. I equated it to climbing a mountain. If you get stuck in the middle, you have to take another route to reach the top. Don't keep trying the same way that you know doesn't work.

My leadership skills were an asset in my beginning the climb. I was used to setting goals and I was not going to fail, but knew I needed to proceed cautiously. Many have said, 'I will never have a drink again' or 'I'll never do drugs," so I learned that it is a 24-hour program. Don't think too far ahead or you set yourself up for failure. This was the counselors' biggest concern with me: they could help sort out my emotions and give me the tools to be successful, but would I turn to something else to fill the void? They had seen it far too often.

It would be a dance that I would have to do for the rest of my life.

After a little time, you make friends and understand that you're all there under similar circumstances.

A hard part for me was, when you talk in a group, you have to give your name and what you are. As an example, "My name is Barry and I am an addict."

I had trouble with this as I was the only one there for a sleeping pill problem. There are addicts of all kinds — heroin, fentanyl, meth, crack, opioids and, yes, sleeping pills. I never had considered myself to be an addict, but my withdrawals were so bad that it only confirmed what I had become.

You eat breakfast and other meals with the same group until someone leaves. The group that I was in, Matt, Mike and David constantly busted each other's balls. It kept you on your toes. I would tell the other guys that I wasn't supposed to be there, that I have a sleeping disorder, but they would shoot that down quickly. Like a prisoner, you think you're innocent; but you're guilty like the rest. Nobody goes to rehab on a winning streak, and the speakers they have come in every day will tell you the same thing. You listen and learn so that's what I did.

There is a lot of crying at rehab because of the loved ones you've hurt — including yourself. Step One of the 12 steps is the hardest for me: surrendering and admitting your life is unmanageable. Yeah, it's a tough one. You give yourself to a higher power. It's not about religion. It's about sanity and you haven't been able to control it.

||| THE CELL |||

There are around 100 people there at any given time and although they keep the genders separated, you find ways to communicate with each other. Everyone there is hurting and shaking their head. You're only human.

After 10 days, you lose track of time. Brookdale is in a beautiful setting and a great place to heal, but at times it does feel like a prison — and that's what I needed: A slap in the head before it was too late.

The biggest kicker of all was that I was in Philadelphia Flyers territory. When a woman was wearing a Flyers t-shirt, it drove me up the wall, but I made my bed so had to take it like a man.

I thought, "At least send me to Rangers country," but that would have been too easy. Climbing the mountain is satisfying if you can reach the top and that is the goal. The struggle along the way only makes you stronger.

My use of sleeping pills does have its repercussions, such as permanent nerve damage. I'm not 20 years old, so my brain takes longer to heal now also.

I've found that laughter is the best policy, be it at yourself or at the expense of someone else. As long as it's not hurtful, everyone is in play at rehab.

One exercise my counselor had me do is called 'the open chair exercise.' You write a letter to a loved one who has passed, then you sit across from the open chair and read the letter as if they are there.

My counselor suggested I write the letter to Mark, as he thought it might be too difficult for Brock.

It *was* tough, but the actual writing of the letter to Mark was a relief.

When I sat across from the open chair and began to read, I struggled to get through it. So much hurt and pain was being released.

It's what I needed.

At times it may have felt like prison, but running out of pills was the best thing that could have happened to me.

I can't thank the staff at Brookdale, the New York Rangers and the NHL Alumni enough for their support and guidance through these turbulent waters.

I will continue to honor my son Brock and good friend Mark, as I feel their spirits close to me. By doing that, I honor myself, and that is the key: Love yourself through trauma and use it for opportunity.

I believe in my faith and dream again. There is a place in the highlands of Scotland. It's a castle on a Loch. I dream of being there. It's at this place where I will meet my son and embrace him in my arms. To die is to live again for eternity.

Elvis Has Left the Building

March, 1982

Bam!! I hit Gaetan Duchesne of the Washington Capitals with a hard bodycheck at center ice with just under 10 seconds to go in the first period. It was a big part of my game: Look for players who have their heads down and aren't paying attention, then read, search and destroy!

The hit was hard enough that he fell backwards, and his leg flew up into the air. As his leg swung around, his skate sliced across my face just under my right eye, starting from my nose in a semicircle two inches past my eye. It was about a 12-inch gash, down to the bone. I could see the blood squirting out before my face went completely numb.

I fell to one knee. The blood continued to pour out, so I put my glove to the area to try and stop the flow.

Trainer Bob Williams was quickly beside me. He cleared my glove away and applied pressure to the wound with a towel to stop the blood flow. He then helped me off the ice and into the dressing room. When we got through to the medical area, Bob sat me on the trainer's table.

When Nick Fotiu came over, I saw his face turn white and knew this wasn't good.

Dr. Norman Scott quickly arrived, and Bob lifted the towel a little to give him a look. Dr. Scott then said, "Bubba, we've got to get you to the hospital!"

The medical staff put me on a gurney and wheeled me down the hallway to the area where the ambulance was waiting. They eased me into the ambulance before securing me.

The ice level is on the fifth floor at Madison Square Garden, and the ambulance is parked by the Zamboni at all times. We began the short winding drive down to street level. The ambulance turned on its flashing lights and siren as we proceeded to Lenox Hill Hospital.

THE CELL

It was a bumpy ride, and I could feel the warm blood filling up my right ear canal. The numbness was wearing off, and I could feel the muscle tissue sliding across my facial bone when a bump in the road moved it.

Speeding from the Garden to Lenox Hill isn't exactly a smooth ride.

I thought, "Am I going to lose my eye?!"

The blood in my ear only accentuated every sound, sort of like a speaker. The whole episode reminded me of a scene from *NYPD Blue!*

Upon arrival at Lenox Hill, I was taken to a room where doctors examined me. Dr. Scott had to stay at the Garden, in case anyone else was injured. The Lenox Hill doctor said after examining the cut, "We're going to have to call in the plastic surgeon specialist from Long Island, Barry, as this is a deep wound where I can see the facial bone around your eye."

Not everyone called me 'Bubba,' a nickname I got from football star Bubba Smith during my high school football days.

An hour and a half later, the plastic surgeon showed up. He looked at the cut before saying, "Oh, yeah! I like this one! I'm going to have you looking pretty in no time!"

I wasn't pretty before, so I thought "Heck! Maybe there's a positive here: I could end up looking like Elvis — the skinny Elvis!"

The doctor began stitching the inside tissue around the bone first. With my ear being plugged with blood, I could hear the needle and thread each time he did a stitch. I began to count.

It was another 90 minutes of lying on the table before all the stitches were done. The doctor then got the staple gun and stapled the cut closed.

Before the procedure, a nurse had removed my right contact lens, as my eye was beginning to close from the trauma that occurred.

The doctor asked me, "Do you know how many stitches and staples I put in?"

"Well, I counted 65 stitches and 12 staples." I replied.

"Wow! You're very close. I put in 67 stitches and 12 staples, so you did get the staples right!"

"Do I look a little like Elvis now?"

He said, "I think you should wait until the morning. You will look different for sure!"

"You're very lucky to still have your eye. An eighth of an inch closer and we'd be doing a different surgery!"

They kept me at the hospital a while longer, with ice packs over my eye, before releasing me. I put my clothes on and went outside to take a taxi back to my condo on East 46th street.

It was there that I first got a look at the damage caused. My eye was almost shut, and it would be completely closed by the morning. I looked more like Herman Munster than Elvis!

The next morning, we were flying to Pittsburgh to play the Penguins that night. I took a taxi out to LaGuardia Airport, where the team had congregated. Everyone was checking out my eye and saying I was better looking now than before. It eased the pain a little. Anything for a laugh when you're traveling with 20 guys.

As we got to the boarding gate, I began to hear whispers and comments like, "Check this out!" I thought they were talking about me. When I looked up there was a beautiful girl in the waiting area of our flight. Girls were the last thing I was thinking about. When you travel with 20 guys, they are still focused and pay attention to all the details just like a game.

Even the coaches were checking her out!

As we boarded the commercial flight, they usually left the middle seat open to make it more comfortable for us. I always sit in the aisle seat, in case anything happens.

After we got settled, the rest of the passengers began to board. Then we saw the girl coming down the aisle, looking up and checking the seat numbers. As she went past Ron Duguay's seat, he shrugged his shoulders in disbelief.

I think this was the only time I didn't want a pretty girl sitting next to me, having to look at my Halloween eye the entire flight. My eye was closed shut and turning blue. It was swollen, with staples protruding and Vaseline covering the wound — I looked sort of like Jake LaMotta after a fight.

I said to myself, "Please, Lord, don't let her sit by me!"

As she finally reached my aisle, I heard, "Excuse me: I'm in the middle seat." As I got up from my seat to let her through, she checked out my eye. Sure enough, she'd be staring at my eye the whole flight. I tried to look away, but the wound covered half my face by now. I thought she would ask the flight attendant to be moved to another seat and was surprised when she started up a conversation with me.

She asked, "If you don't mind, what happened to your eye?"

After the shock subsided, I began to tell her the story of the incident.

We talked the whole hour to Pittsburgh. She told me she was modeling down in Pitt for two days. I asked, "Have you ever seen a hockey game?"

"No," she replied, "I haven't."

I thought to myself, "Come on, boy! You can do this!"

"Would you like to come to the game tonight?" I asked.

She said "Can you play with your eye closed and hurt?"

"I'm going to try," I replied.

We landed in Pittsburgh and said our goodbyes. I gave her my phone number in New York and told her I would leave her two tickets at will call under her name.

We dropped off our gear at "The Igloo," Pittsburgh Civic Center, and headed across the street to the hotel for our pre-game meal and afternoon rest. I couldn't sleep all day and headed to the rink early for the 7:30 game.

THE CELL

Trainer Jerry "Haggie" Maloney had fixed a visor onto my helmet to protect my eye, but this wasn't going to be easy. I only had vision in one eye with a contact lens in. It was difficult to focus, and I began to get a migraine headache.

Haggie said, "Maybe you shouldn't be playing this game, Bubba."

We needed the two points, so there was never a question if I would play or not.

Haggie said, "Let's see after warm-ups."

When I got out for warmups, I thought I was going to vomit. Between the migraine and everything else, I surely wouldn't be playing in the modern game. But the 80's were different.

After warmup, Haggie asked me, "Well, how do you feel?"

"Never felt better. Good to go," I said. The coaches left it up to the trainers, and the trainers left it up to the players, so I was going to at least try to play.

I said to myself just try and play simple, but that wasn't my game. I had to have a physical presence and play a power game to be effective.

During my first shift, I was in front of our net when the puck was passed out of the corner to the player beside me. I didn't even see him before he scored. My second shift, I knew I had to move my head around to have any vision at all.

I played what I thought was a one-on-one from center, but it was actually a two-on-one. The Penguins player passed it through my legs to his teammate and it was in the net. It was 2-0 for Pittsburgh and I was minus-2 on my two shifts.

Coach Herb Brooks said to me, "Bubba, that's it for tonight."

I sat on the bench the rest of the period. As soon as the period ended, I got undressed, showered, then put my clothes on and watched the rest of the game in the tunnel area.

We ended up losing the game. I lost some of my eyesight temporarily, lost the girl and damn near lost my mind!!

Would my eye be OK? Would we make the playoffs? Would I ever see the girl again? Sorry I can't say her name now.

It was only the start of having over 200 stitches in my face and head during a 10-year NHL career. The physical pain you can deal with, but the emotional pain can last forever.

Creed

April, 1971

Growing up in Vancouver, I was around sports daily. If you grow up on the playground, you're going to be tough or you don't play.

The PNE grounds were part of our East Van 'hood.' They had the Vancouver Canucks of the Western League playing out of the Forum, and the BC Lions, who played out of Empire Stadium — made famous by the 1954 Commonwealth Games' "Miracle Mile" with Roger Bannister passing John Landy on the last lap to win. It was the first time two runners had finished the mile in under four minutes in the same race.

I worked for the Lions as a ball boy from 1969-71. I had a chance to see what it was like to be a pro athlete. I was in the dressing room for practices and on the sidelines for games. I was in the film room with coach Jackie Parker and watched the players prepare to do battle. They were tough, and there was a lot of blood and broken limbs that trainer Rocky Cavallin had to take care of.

There, I learned what tough was. Play with blood, sweat and more blood!

In 1971 a new player joined the team after being released from the Oakland Raiders. His name was Carl Weathers, and when he took his shirt off at the first practice, there were a lot of jaws that dropped. In the words of Robert Downey Jr. (Kirk Lazarus) from the movie Tropic Thunder "He's more ripped than a Julienne Salad!" Carl was in awesome shape and a lot of guys immediately were in the weight room after practice.

I was only 13, but Carl took a liking to me and I filled him in on all the players. He said, "I don't know how long I'm going to be here, but while I'm here, we're going to be good friends." I liked the sound of that.

He would get tested his very first practice from one of my idols, Jim Young. 'Younger' was a Canadian slotback/flanker and also played some defense at times. He was a tough SOB, and you had to know where he was on the field at all times. I saw him forearm and knock out a lot of DB's that weren't paying attention. They didn't call him "Dirty Thirty" for nothing, referring to the number 30 he wore.

The offense was running plays and Carl was watching them closely. I was there beside him, as I was for most scrimmages. When coach Parker said "Weathers, you're in!" he grabbed his helmet and said, "Time to make something happen!" and that he did.

He lined up at his outside linebacker position and was ready. The ball was snapped and it was a quick little look-in crossing pass to Jim Young.

Carl read the play and the two of them met like the running of the bulls — Jim with his elbows up and Carl throwing all his muscles into the heavy collision. Now this was football!

Carl's helmet popped off and the two went down throwing punches.

They let them go for a while before players and coaches broke them up. Coach Parker called the rest of the practice off.

Carl had earned some respect and Jim had kept his.

After playing a few games for the Lions, Carl told me he was thinking of going back to San Diego to study acting. There were already some players trying to cross over, as Jim Brown did.

I came to practice one day and Carl's gear was gone from his locker.

Everyone said he'd gone back down south.

A few months later, I saw him in an episode of the cop show "Kojak," playing a bad guy.

Then, the next month, he was in "Mannix," another cop show. I didn't hear too much of him after that.

Then heard about this new movie, "Rocky."

Everyone said you got to check out "Apollo Creed." So I watched the movie, and Apollo Creed was played by Carl Weathers. He had gotten his big break. Went on to star in "Predator" and "Happy Gilmore" among others.

I learned a valuable lesson from Carl Weathers: Fight for what you believe in. Same as what he had told me as a starry-eyed teenager.

Been trying to do that ever since.

When the Redbird Sings

September, 1974

It was a goal of mine to play Junior hockey for Ernie "Punch" McLean and the New Westminster Bruins.

I would go watch their games at Queen's Park Arena in 'New West' and thought these games are better than the NHL as far as entertainment.

Queen's Park was located right behind the BC Maximum Security Prison known as "The BC Pen." It was an uneasy feeling for teams to come in off the freeway by bus and drive by "The Pen" before turning into Queen's Park.

Frequent guests to the games were handcuffed inmates, longshoremen, and Hells Angels members that liked to sit behind the opposing team's net. If they weren't scared before, they sure were now. There were also loyal fans in 'New West' known as the Royal City.

I was playing Tier Two Junior for Langley Lords, which was the Kamloops' Chiefs farm team, and my brother Murray played for the Bruins.

Bellingham, USA were the Bruins' farm team, and I knew them well, as we were in the same league and rivals. Bellingham had some great players like Stan Smyl, Brad Maxwell, Kevin Schamehorn, Harold Phillipoff, Miles Zaharko, Randy Rudnyk and Carey Walker in goal.

My brother Murray had played for the Vancouver Nats in the WCHL, like the Bruins, but he said assistant coach Jack Durston didn't like him so he was released and caught on with Ernie and the Bruins.

The only hockey school I ever went to was run by Jack Durston out of Kerrisdale Arena in Vancouver, and he gave me all "C's" on my report card, so I didn't like him, either. Probably was a nice man but that's hockey!

THE CELL

New Westminster is only 20 minutes from Vancouver and Langley another 20 minutes from there. It was easy for me to go to Bruins games. I loved their aggressive style of play.

My brother mentioned to Ernie that he thought I was going to be a good player, so Ernie came out to Langley to watch me play. Murray called me and said, "Make sure you do something tonight, because Ernie is coming to watch you play."

So I did. I got in three fights with Harold Phillipoff, who Ernie loved. I fought him on the ice and then again in the penalty box twice before being ejected from the game.

Murray called me the next day and said, "Wow! Ernie really likes you and wants to make a trade for you!"

I loved hearing that.

Ernie met with my parents confidentially and asked them to write a letter to then-commissioner Ed Chynoweth of the Western Canada Hockey League (WCHL), explaining how they wanted me to play close to home, as they were worried about my schooling. Kamloops was a four-hour drive from Vancouver, and that's where I would have played.

Kamloops had to go along with commissioner Chynoweth's request. I was traded for the first time for five players and was now a Bruin.

In September of 1975 we met at Queen's Park Arena, and the new team Ernie had assembled took the bus to Westlock, Alberta, where we would have our training camp. We all got to know one another on the bus trip and I was now playing with some tough and talented hockey players.

I always wanted to play for Ernie, and now was my chance. We were well into training camp when our first exhibition game was coming up against the Edmonton Oil Kings at the Edmonton Gardens.

The day before the game, Ernie called me in after practice for a meeting. He said "Bubba, you're probably going to be in this league for three years, so tomorrow night would be a good time to make a statement."

"Okay, Punch. No problem," I replied.

I told some of the guys what Ernie had said to me as we gathered around and was asked, "What does that mean?"

Harold Phillipoff said, "That means Bubba's gonna kill someone tomorrow night. Haha!" as only some laughed.

We got on the bus the next day and headed to Edmonton. I was all wound up as it was a quiet ride thinking about the events that would take place. All that went through my mind was, "Make a statement!" If Ernie told you to do something, you happily did it.

We got dressed for the game and I was ready. When they opened up the gates I went flying out onto the ice and did a hard lap around the ice.

As I went by the Edmonton bench I heard a guy yelling at me "Hey, Beck, we're gonna get you tonight!"

I turned, looked back and there was a guy behind the Edmonton bench. I continued on and the next time by he said the same thing, "Beck, we're getting you tonight!"

By the time I got to the other side of the rink, I snapped. Here goes the statement Ernie was talking about. I made a bee-line for the guy behind the bench with my stick already in a spearing position. I put all my weight into the first spear. After he went down, I continued spearing him a few times then punched him in the head with my glove still on. By that time, all the other players had come over and were pairing up and tugging each other every which way. The officials came over and finally broke everything up and sent both teams off the ice.

I heard my teammates say, "That's it, Bubba! Way to kick his ass!" We were now in our dressing room, congratulating each other, and the game hadn't even started yet. It was our first test as a team. I was feeling pretty good about my statement when the dressing room door opened.

Ernie stuck his head in and said "Barry, can you come out and see me please?" Guys were patting me on the back as I went out the door.

Ernie led me down a hallway away from the dressing room before turning around and saying, "Bubba, I said make a statement."

"I thought I did, Ernie."

Ernie said "That guy you speared is Redbird!"

"Okay" I replied.

"No, it's not okay," Ernie said, before going on to explain that Redbird, who had intellectual disabilities, had been the stickboy here for twenty years!

"What? I didn't know that Ernie. I was just making a statement." All I could think was, 'My mother's going to kill me!'

Ernie said, "You have to go apologize to him."

"Yes. No problem, Ernie."

I felt terrible. Mental disabilities? Oh my god!

Ernie took me down to Edmonton's dressing room and knocked on the door. Ernie looked in and coach Hodge came out with Redbird. He had a big smile on his face which was already bruising up. I apologized to him and gave him my stick. He said, "I told you we were going to get you, Beck."

I had to admire his wisdom, as the coaches smiled.

"Can we be friends, Redbird? I'd like that" I asked.

He said "Sure, Beck," and I shook his hand.

Ernie walked me back to the dressing room.

When I went inside, everyone asked me what happened.

"The guy I speared is Redbird, the 45-year-old stickboy!" I said.

THE CELL

Everyone started laughing. I didn't mention his disability. I was still worried what my mom and dad were going to say — especially that my mom was a nurse.

"What kind of a son have I raised," I could hear her say.

Two nights later, we went back to Edmonton as Westlock wasn't too far. Everyone reminded me before the game to leave Redbird alone.

As we went out onto the ice for warmup, I could see Redbird at Edmonton's bench with this huge down jacket on for protection. As I came towards him, he pointed at his jacket and with a serious face said, "Can't get me now, Beck!" and smiled. I shook his hand again and would every time we played Edmonton for the next three years. He even stopped calling me "Beck" and used "Barry," so I knew we were friends.

For the next three years, I would find out there were a few more mentally challenged stick boys around the league but decided it would be better to shake their hand instead of spearing them!

Sonny and The King

December, 1979

When I was traded to the Rangers from Colorado I just simply moved my gear to the visitors' dressing room as the Rangers were in town.

Before the game I met my new teammates and tried to get acclimated but was nervous as all hell being now the adversary in my own rink.

When coach Fred Shero announced the starting lineup, he said "Ok, Espo at center, Maloney on right wing and Hitch (Pat Hickey) on the left side."

Espo had to correct him and say "Freddie, we traded Hitch yesterday for Barry Beck, who's playing with us tonight."

"Oh yeah. That's right," as we all had a good laugh.

That was the last laugh had all night, as I was an emotional mess before this game. Colorado came out flying and I think the final was 7-2 Colorado as most of the players I was traded for were on the scoreboard.

We left the next day for Vancouver. I was going back to my hometown, but this time I was playing for the Rangers.

I felt a little more comfortable this game and we won, 4-2. Our house was only one block away from the Pacific Coliseum, so had a chance to visit mom and dad and celebrate a little as they were excited for the opportunity that was being presented to me.

The next day, we took the return flight back to NYC. As we flew over the city, I got my first good look at The Big Apple. I thought the Rangers are an 'Original Six' team and hadn't won the Stanley Cup in a long time. There was going to be a lot of pressure on me that would come with the territory. I said to myself, "We must win!"

I knew Ron Greschner, so he said I could sleep on his couch until I found my own place.

||| THE CELL |||

The next day would be my first game playing for the Rangers at Madison Square Garden.

I didn't sleep much, but when I got to the Garden, I was pumped. We were playing L.A. and I wanted to set a high standard and try and achieve that every game. Consistency is law if you want to be good!

When I came into the dressing room and saw my jersey in my locker, I was stoked.

I did my pre-game rituals as always, putting on my left skate first then a short prayer. Then it was time to go. Had a decent warm-up but noticed the sightlines were different. Every rink was different, and if you weren't comfortable with the sightlines, you were in trouble. The ice was a little soft but that was standard for the Garden. I actually loved it, but it would take me time to get a feel for "The Garden Experience!"

When you're in the starting lineup, standing on the blue line for the National Anthem, playing in front of 20,000 fans, it will get your heart pumping!! It's a harsh adrenaline rush! The Garden is a magical place, and I wanted to start banging bodies as soon as the puck was dropped.

During the first period, Phil Esposito was carrying the puck up center ice when I jumped into the play. I caught up to him and broke down the left wing. He feathered me a nice soft pass over the defenseman's stick, and as I received it, I cut in around the defenseman. As I got closer to the net, Kings goalie Ron Grahame came sliding out, but I managed to flip the puck over him while catapulting myself up on to the crossbar of the net.

The puck was in the net and it felt unbelievable with the crowd cheering. It was probably the best goal I ever scored in my whole life but still have never seen the video of it.

I thought I had a great game and afterwards all the boys said, "We're taking the limo and heading to "54," as in *Studio 54*.

Before that, we all met downstairs at *Charley O's*. The restaurant was filled with fans, so we managed to all squeeze into a back booth. Espo, Ron Duguay, Don Murdoch, Gresch and me – all the boys who lived in the city.

We grabbed some cold ones and then noticed Sonny Werblin, the man behind the Rangers and Knicks, sitting in the corner with someone who looked like boxing promoter Don King.

We all went over and paid our respects, then went back to our booth. By this time, the whole restaurant was paying attention, as that's what they came down for: excitement and meeting the players.

All of a sudden, Don King stands up and starts yelling from across the room. "Bubba Beck: 'Too Tall' wants you!"

Now, I'm a boxing fan and knew Ed "Too Tall" Jones had played defensive end for the Dallas Cowboys and was now trying his hand at the sweet science.

Ron Duguay said, "You got to say something back," as we were all laughing.

Don King wouldn't stop. "Oh yeah, Bubba: me and Sonny talking right now about you and 'Too Tall!'"

OK, I guess this is what happens in NYC!!

I yelled back to Don, "Bring 'Too Tall' on, Don. Bring him on!" Don kept going on for about 10 minutes, back-and-forth banter that I was going to enjoy. We finished our beer, went over to say goodnight and Don said, "Me and Sonny talking money now, Bubba. You gonna love it!"

We jumped into our limo and headed to "54." There was a huge crowd outside, but when we got out of the limo, door manager Mark Benecke met us outside and the crowd parted as we went in. Mark was a big hockey fan and told me, "Any time you want to come down, Barry, let me know." and handed me his card. I ended up using that card more than I should have, but this was NYC in the 80's!!

Sonny Werblin liked players being seen in the city clubs and restaurants, so that's what we did. He used to be Joe Namath's agent.

As we went into Studio it was the first time I'd ever seen co-ed bathrooms. There were couches and chairs in there, people making out and the party was happening.

I can't get that night out of my mind, as we partied until the wee hours as studio rocked!!

Sonny and the King: Entertainment at its finest.

Knockout

January, 1983

I was maybe 10 or 11 when I got my hands on an old Sports Illustrated magazine.

I used to love the old photos of all the athletes.

Sports Illustrated and hockey magazines were all that caught my attention until I found my oldest brother's Playboy under his bed by mistake. It sure beat looking at National Geographic!

Out of all the photos in S.I., there was one that caught my attention and would stick in my mind for a long time. That was a photo of "The Man," Walt 'Clyde the Glide' Frazier.

He played for the Knicks, and I thought NYC must be a cool place if Clyde is there.

The photo was of him with a long fur coat, plaid pants, white turtleneck, gold chain around his neck with a wide-brimmed hat on, basketball in hand — all while standing in front of his Rolls Royce. He reminded me of "Huggy Bear" from "Starsky and Hutch!"

If I ever made pro, I wanted to at least dress like Clyde and have that cool pro vibe that he had. It wouldn't be easy to reach that level of coolness. For now, it was just another dream coming down the pipeline in a young boy's head.

After I got settled into living in NYC, Espo, Gresch, Doogs and Doc would take me around to the trendiest shops to look for some cool threads. It usually meant snakeskin boots, tight corduroy pants with a wacked-out shirt and jacket. I'd think, 'Could I ever reach 'Clyde' status?' It was 'shop till you drop' after most practices.

We had a road game in Chicago and Espo said on the flight going there, "I got this guy that my brother, Tony, knows that sells fur coats. He's going to bring some by the hotel when we get in."

Damn! My mother had a mink coat back in the day that she inherited from her mom. I would try it on and think I was "Clyde," but it wasn't ankle-length like his.

We got to the hotel in Chicago and around an hour later, my phone rings and it's Espo.

THE CELL

"Bubba come meet me in fifteen minutes on the 10th floor. The furs are here!"

I think I was there in five minutes and knocked on the door.

Espo answered with a big grin on his face and said, "Come on in, my man!" I was the first one there and met the guy who had two, big, long cases with him. That had to be the furs, I thought.

"Let's wait for the other guys" Espo said.

The salesman said, "Phil, I can open these up and let Barry have a look." Phil replied, "Ok, let's do it!"

Doogs, Gresch and Doc would have to get there fast, as I was excited to get a glimpse inside those cases.

He opened the first case and my eyes bugged out of my head. A long row of furs in lots of dark and multi-colors. The salesman did his pitch when there was a knock at the door. The rest of the guys came in and were just as excited as me. It was -25 outside and cold back in New York, too, so a fur coat seemed like the way to go. When the salesman opened up the second case, we were in shock as we now settled in with a glass of whiskey.

These were prime furs, and we tried to take our time, but we couldn't take it any longer.

The salesman said, "Barry I got something for you that you're going to love!" The other guys were still looking in the first case. The salesman pulls out this ankle-length, brown fur coat with a high neck. I tried it on and it fit perfectly. When I looked in the mirror, I could see 'Clyde.'

Doc said, laughing, "Oh, Bubba. That's you!"

Everyone else tried on different furs as I walked around with my whiskey, thinking how far I'd come from a young boy in Vancouver. This wasn't my mother's mink anymore. This was the real deal!

"Barry this coat was made for you!" the salesman said. "What's it made of?" I asked.

"Otter," he replied.

A full-length otter coat. Now at that time, I wasn't thinking how many otters were killed to make the coat; I had already fallen in love with it. Furs were another element of fashion that weren't frowned upon as they are today.

After everyone had the jacket they wanted, the salesman asked, "Well, do you want the good news?"

We all looked at each other like there wasn't going to be any good news when a salesman says that. He started giving out the prices. There was silence when he rolled out the numbers. I only remember that when he got to me and said, "Barry, the otter is ten thousand."

Ten grand! Wow! I took one last look in the mirror and I thought what would Clyde do? "Sure. I'll take it." It didn't matter how many otters it took; if you wanted to look like Clyde, you had to let it roll.

Back then, I always brought my checkbook with me, as I didn't have a credit card yet and cut the check. It hurt, but I wanted that fur so bad to finally look like a pro should look. We were all jumping around in the room like elementary school kids. Laughing and kidding one another. Espo had set us up real good.

A couple of years later we were playing in Toronto. There was always a big rivalry on our team from players who were from Western Canada and players who were from Eastern Canada. Toronto was the haven for Eastern Canadian boys. A lot of their parents came to the games in Toronto as ours did out west in Vancouver, Calgary and Edmonton.

Playing in the Maple Leaf Gardens had a lot of history, so it was another game where you had to be ready. It was the day before the "Super Bowl," so there was a lot of media attention surrounding this game. Late in the first period the puck was in Toronto's end when it was shot out while I was pinching down on the play. It was now a race for the puck between me and the Leafs forward. We were both skating hard after the puck as we could see it wasn't going to be icing. The puck slowly stopped around the face-off dot in our end. I was just about to get to the puck first when our goalie Glen Hanlon came flying out of his crease pads-first.

I didn't see him and crashed over top before being catapulted into the end boards head-first at full speed. I didn't wear a helmet, so I immediately blacked out and laid on the ice. I didn't know if I broke my neck; all I knew was this is what it feels like to be "Knocked Out!"

It was only four or five seconds, but when I came to, I didn't know where we were. Our trainer Jerry (Haggie) Maloney came out, as now I could also hear Glen Hanlon asking, "Bubba, Bubba are you okay?" I slowly came around and realized that I hadn't broken my neck. Jerry attended to me and with some help from other players I managed to get up and off the ice just behind our net where the gate was to our dressing room. Once in the room, Toronto doctors were already waiting to examine me. After a couple of minutes I heard them say, "Okay let's get him to the hospital."

They put me on a gurney and took me to the waiting ambulance. I was on my way to the hospital when I remembered I was having a Super Bowl party at my place in NYC and had a lot of people coming. How was I ever going to make it?

The team was chartering out, as it was only an hour flight back to NYC. Once at the hospital, I was told I would be staying overnight as they had to run some tests on me. That would include an MRI and being awakened every 45 minutes. The doctors were concerned for any brain swelling or other trauma. I didn't care about that; I only was thinking about the party.

By the time Haggie made it to the hospital, I had somewhat regained my senses. I told him "Haggie, I've got a Super Bowl party at my place tomorrow!" He said, "Don't worry. If you're okay, you can fly out in the morning and still make the party. I'll be staying overnight with you." I felt relieved but would be doing tests all night and wouldn't be getting any sleep.

Doing the brain MRI was a whole other experience. You're tightly packed, lying down in a cubicle and can't move. There is a constant knocking noise and it feels like you're about to be shot into outer space. It took around 30 minutes, then it was back to my room — to be woken up the rest of the night.

In the morning, Haggie came and the doctors re-examined me before saying that they would like me to stay for a couple of days. I wasn't having any of that, and told them I felt fine and had to get back to NYC. Through some discussions with Haggie, the doctors finally said I could leave. I could still make the 10:30 am flight back and host the party!

I was dizzy on the flight but just excited to be going home. Upon landing, I got a taxi from LaGuardia to my place, where friends were already setting up for the party. I put on my fur coat – and sunglasses, as I had an atrium in my condo and all the light was giving me a headache.

The guests were arriving and the food was all laid out, so it was time to party. The bathtub was full of ice and beer and the game was about to begin.

I lived in an old manufacturer's building that had been turned into condos and it was a cool place to live. There were photographers, models and even Irene Cara from "Fame" lived on my floor.

The game was going on and there were lots of people coming and going as most were from my building.

At one point a guy came up to me and said, "Is your name Barry?"

"Yes" I replied.

"I'm here to pick up the stuff and move it to Florida tomorrow."

I said "What?"

"The stuff" he said. "Man, I don't know what you're talking about. I'm just having a party here. If you want something to eat, go ahead."

He then said "This is condo 17D, correct?"

I said, "Yes but I don't know you, man. I think you got the wrong place."

"Your name is Barry Greene, is it not?" "F..k no brother. You got the wrong place!"

I took him down the hall and called the doorman on the intercom. "Cortez, you sent some guy up to my party and he's looking for Barry Greene."

"Sorry Mr. Beck, Barry Greene lives in 7D — not 17D like you."

"Buddy you're in the wrong place." I told him.

He left and I never saw him again. I didn't ever meet Barry Greene and left a note for all the doormen to please send people to the right places.

The Super Bowl was a blowout and over by halftime. I had a headache the rest of the day. When everyone had helped clean up and left, I looked in the mirror with my fur coat and sunglasses. I thought, 'Man, there's only one Clyde! Just one!!'

Don't Cry For Me

January, 1983

By the time the 82-83 season rolled around, I was making NYC my permanent home. I lived near the U.N. on 46th St. and enjoyed traveling out to Northport, L.I. during the summer months to visit my good friend Rob Ingraham and his wife, June.

Rob had been instrumental in helping me adjust to NYC and become more focused as captain of the team. I will be forever grateful to him and June for their acceptance of me.

While I wanted to do Penthouse Pet lingerie shows, Rob helped me set up a foundation through the United Neighborhood Houses of New York. We brought underprivileged kids from Harlem, the Bronx, Queens and the Lower East Side to Ranger games at MSG. Normally, they'd never get the opportunity, so I met the kids after games and they never pulled any punches with their questions. True New Yorkers!

I enjoyed this part of living in NY: connecting with people, staying grounded and being committed to the cause. I also liked to have fun! I ended up doing the Penthouse show anyway (what red-blooded Canadian kid wouldn't?), and am still friends with one of the girls today. That show is a whole other chapter unto itself!

You, of course, meet a lot of celebrities because you travel in the same circles. Trendy restaurants and clubs are where models and athletes hook up. It was a common theme in the 80's and probably still is, but social media has now changed the game.

During the '82-83 season, I was friendly with Patti Lupone, who starred in "Evita" on Broadway. She would sometimes sing the National Anthem before our games. When I had friends come down from Vancouver and we would go see her perform, she would send them up to see the lighting controller, and he would let them work the lights for her show.

They got a big kick out of that.

||| THE CELL |||

She also happened to grow up in Northport with Rob Ingraham, and that's how we met.

After Patti finished her run in "Evita," she went down to Philly to shoot a movie. We happened to be playing the Flyers in a home-and-home series on Saturday afternoon and Sunday night back at the Garden. I contacted Patti; she had some work to do and couldn't make the afternoon game, but would meet us afterward. There was a bar near the Spectrum, so Patti told me, "I'll pick you guys up at your hotel, then we'll go have a drink."

Usually, we would bus straight back to Rye after the game, but the coaches elected to go back in the morning and rest up for Sunday night's game.

We beat Philly, so everyone was in a pretty good mood. We bused back to the hotel, where Patti had said she would pick us up in her new red Volkswagen Cabriolet. She loved that car.

Eddie Mio, Pierre Larouche and myself waited in the lobby and watched the rain pouring down outside. As Patti pulled up, Nick Fotiu and some of the other players were just coming out of the elevator.

We went outside and jumped into Patti's car with the rain pouring down all around us. As Nicky opened up the hotel door, we motioned to him to jump in but then Patti didn't see him and took off with Nick standing in the rain. This was not good because Nicky was going to get you back twice as bad for something like that. He pulled his practical jokes most of the year, so we figured we all owed him at least one good laugh. Nick only saw it as, "He who laughs last wins!!"

We all met up at the bar with Patti and when Nicky came up he said, "You guys are a bunch of funny guys now, aren't you!" We laughed, but his laugh was different. We had to be on our toes now.

We had a couple of drinks, then Patti told us she knew this great diner where we could eat. She wrote down the name and directions and gave it to Ron Greschner.

Eddie, Pierre and I drove with Patti and were first at the diner. She parked her new car in the back, out of sight from everyone — or so we thought. We settled into a window booth where we could see everyone come in. Nicky and the boys came in shortly thereafter with big grins on their faces. This was not good.

They were laughing all through the meal. We were the first ones to finish, as Patti had to get back to her hotel because she was shooting in the morning. When we got up to leave, Nicky said, "Enjoy the ride home!" That made me a little nervous.

We walked to the back of the diner, then got our first glimpse of Patti's car. There was the diner's garbage piled six feet high on top of her car! Rotten lettuce, what looked like Thousand Island dressing, french fries and all the rest of the garbage, from one end of the car to the other.

We looked at Patti, and she was in tears. We consoled her, then started removing the garbage. Eddie was dry heaving, as it must have been all week's garbage. Pierre continued removing the movr and I went back inside and got a towel.

"Good one Nicky," I said as he replied again, "Enjoy the ride!"

Now, we're teammates. We don't get into fights over these kinds of things; you just try to one-up the other guy next time, as it makes for a fun year. It was not fun for Patti, though.

We finally got her car cleared off and I toweled it down best I could.

She even drove us back to hotel, tears still flowing.

When we finally got back to NYC, I called Rob Ingraham and told him what happened to Patti's car and that Nicky as usual was the ringleader. He phoned me back an hour later.

"Okay this is what we're going to do. I'm going to put a legal document together saying that there was over $6,000 damage to Patti's car and she is going to file a civil suit against Nicky. I will give the letter to one of the stickboys after warmup at tonight's game." Oh yeah, I liked the sound of this!

Nicky did his usual preparation before a game of looking in the mirror and applying Vaseline like a boxer. Since we were playing the Flyers, it could come in handy. I used a little myself at times.

Nick was pacing back and forth in the dressing room, so I knew this was going to be good. He was going through his pre-game preps, then out the door we went.

After warmup, I came off before Nick so I could take in everything that was about to happen. Nicky came in a minute later, sweating and jacked to play the Flyers. We all were.

Nicky was standing in the middle of the dressing room, having a sport drink, when I saw the stickboy come in with the letter.

I watched Nicky take the letter from him, and say, "What the heck is this?"

It's only 10 minutes before the game, and he was pissed.

He took the letter and went back in the trainer's room. I could hear him cursing as he began to read. I had told Eddie and Pierre about the letter before the game so we were trying our best not to laugh or it would be a long year!

Nicky finally came out of the trainer's room and said, "Anyone know anything about this letter?"

"What kind of letter?" Gresch asked.

By now, Nicky's irate, as he's trying to get ready for the Flyers. He threw the letter on the table and loudly said in his best Staten Island accent: "She's gonna be singing at the bottom of the East River when I get done with her!!"

The tables had turned, and this is the way it was with Nick. He loved keeping the team loose, but it was always hilarious when someone tried to get him back. You never ever fell asleep on a plane, bus or train after that, as you knew Nick was there, lurking in the shadows, ready to pounce! Nick was loved by everyone and a great teammate!

Pepe Comes to Broadway

December, 1983

In the summer of 1983, the Rangers were looking to add some vital scoring touch and found it in Pierre (Lucky) Larouche. He was picked up from Hartford as an unrestricted free agent after refusing to sign a termination contract.

Pierre, who also goes by the nickname "Pepe," from his French-Canadian heritage, was a pure goal scorer. They don't come along very often. He was a 94-goal producer for the Sorel Black Hawks of the Quebec Major Junior Hockey League in 1973-74 and was Pittsburgh's first pick, eighth overall, in the 1974 draft.

In his second year with the Penguins, he scored 53 goals and became a local legend before moving on to score 50 goals again with the Canadiens while playing alongside his idol, Guy Lafleur.

Fifty goals with two different teams already. How do you pass on a guy like that?

We heard that he had some problems in Hartford. A sore back and management issues left him available, and New York was where he needed to be.

Some teams think French-Canadian players are insecure, especially that most are located in the Canadian province of Quebec. Quebec is a beautiful province and is the closest thing to being in Europe without actually going there. They constantly want to play politics and have talked for years about separating from Canada to no avail.

I didn't care at all about that. If he was healthy and could help the team, then as captain, I would assist him with any issues he had and expect the rest of the players to do the same. We had a good group of guys, so I knew Pierre would fit in … but I didn't know exactly how.

"Just score, Pierre," I thought.

One thing I do know is a lot of French Canadians have their names on the Stanley Cup! Hockey is a religion in Quebec!

When Pierre came to training camp in '83, he was in good shape.

||| THE CELL |||

Coach Herb Brooks called me into his office and said, "Bubba, I'd like you to take Pierre under your wing and make him feel welcome."

"Sure, Herb. No problem," I replied.

Pierre was introduced to the players before practice and made himself at home. When a pure goal scorer comes in, it makes some guys a little nervous as their jobs are now on the line.

"Pepe" was a player who could give us a long playoff run if we could get by the Islanders.

As we got on the ice for practice, Herb called me over and asked if I would drive Pierre back to Manhattan after practice. Pierre had been staying at a hotel on 53rd St. I was living on East 46th St., so it would give us time to talk on the way in from our practice facility in Rye, N.Y..

During our ride, we discussed his time in Hartford, and how they felt he wasn't a two-way player and his heart wasn't there. When your team doesn't want you, it hurts.

I said, "You have a chance to turn it all around and be a 50-goal scorer again! To be able to accomplish that at the Garden and be the first player in history to score 50 goals with three different teams would be insane!"

He felt unwanted in Hartford but now became excited at this new opportunity. I further went on to say how well the players are treated here and all the fringe benefits that go along with playing for the Rangers.

I told him, "We never stand in line for anything. Clubs, restaurants, concerts … even the police don't give us tickets!

"We have it great here. Now all we have to do is win a Cup!"

Sometimes players need a change of scenery, and to get a chance to play in the "Big Apple" is nothing short of electric. I said, "It's like we've been waiting for you."

I turned onto Central Park West at around 4:30 pm. I would have to turn down 7th Ave. to get to 53rd St., but the sign read, "No turns between 4:00 - 6:00 pm."

Pierre said, "I think it's 'no turn' here, Barry." I made the turn, anyway, and when we got to 57th street a cop in his brown traffic uniform stepped out into my lane and waved me over the curb.

57th and 7th Ave is one of the busier intersections in Manhattan. Instantly, a crowd began to form. Well, I guess now Pierre would get a chance to see how things went down in NYC.

The cop tapped on the driver's side window of my black Volkswagen GTI and asked me for my license and registration. He said, "You know you made an illegal turn onto 7th Avenue, don't you?"

"Yes, officer. I'm just dropping off a friend at his hotel on 53rd."

The cop looked over at Pierre and gave him a double-take. He checked him over pretty good.

The officer took my license, stepped back onto the sidewalk, with the crowd now getting bigger, and began writing me a ticket. At this point, Pierre opened his passenger door and began to step out of the car.

I said, quietly, "Pierre where are you going? You can't be doing that, man. You're going to get arrested!"

Pierre walked towards the cop as their eyes met for the third time. "Excuse me, sir, but do you know who this is?" now pointing at me, sitting in the car.

I cringed, waiting to see what would happen next. The officer looked at my name on my license, then looked at me and said to Pierre, "No, I don't know him."

Pierre said, "This is Barry Beck, captain of the New York Rangers!"

'Ahhhhhhhhhh, where can I hide?' I thought. All this talk I'd been telling Pierre on the way in, and now this!

The cop then looked at my license and said "Barry Beck … Barry Beck … Nope, can't say that I know him, but I do watch a lot of Islander games."

Shot right through the heart!

The cop then asked Pierre what his name was.

"I'm Pierre Larouche," he said proudly.

"Pierre Larouche," the cop said. "Come on: you really Pierre Larouche?!"

"Yes, sir" Pierre responded.

"Damn! I watch you all the time. Love the way you score goals!"

Okay what the hell is going on here?

The cop then walked over to Pierre and shook his hand. Not only that, but a few bystanders also asked him for his autograph.

Then the cop said, "Can I get one of those too?"

I was going to give him two: a right and a left!

The cop then came to my widow and handed me my license back before saying, "I'm not going to give you a ticket today, but please pay attention to the signs, sir."

"Well, yes, officer. I'll make sure I do that," I replied.

Pierre then got back into the car and said, "If you need any help while I'm here, Barry, just let me know."

"I'll let you know, all right," I said as we burst out laughing all the way to his 53rd St. Hotel.

It would be the start of a friendship that still lasts until today.

Pierre went on to score 48 goals with the Rangers, just missing 50 with two games left. He hit posts in those last two games and it sure would have been nice to see him hit the mark.

Pure goal scorers don't come around often like the Bossys, the Middletons and the Kurris, all in that era. I got to play against all of them — Pierre included. Simply put, he was a "Marvel."

"Father Time"

February, 1990

I first met Gloria in Denver while playing for the Colorado Rockies. It was a night of checking out the local bars and I ended up at "The Lyft." I grabbed a Coors from the bar and made my way up the three-floor complex.

On the top floor I had a good look around and directly across from me I set my eyes on her. Now that I had turned pro, I had a little more confidence than I had when I played junior hockey. I could now even approach girls if the circumstances were right.

I walked over to her and asked her "How's your night was going?" She told me, "Someone had recommended I should come here."

After we introduced ourselves, I asked her if she wanted to sit at the bar and have a drink.

Now, I wasn't the smoothest dude at 20 years old, but you have to start somewhere. The more we talked, the more she opened up to me. She was from St. Louis and was here looking at some bands. She knew this is what she wanted to do as a profession, and I admired that she had goals.

I told her, "I know a few other places close by, one being "The Mining Company" and another called "The London House." We hit both of them and were enjoying each other's company. She was leaving the next day to go back to St. Louis. I told her I could give her a ride to the airport, but she had a meeting in the morning and would go to the airport straight from the meeting.

At the entrance of "The London House," owner Bill Hogan had put some of our hockey schedules out for the year. A lot of players used to go there — even on the visiting teams. I looked at one of the schedules and saw where we would be going to St.Louis in a couple of weeks and I had great chemistry with her or else it was the peppermint schnapps. I asked her if I could give her a ride back to her hotel.

THE CELL

She was all business and said she would take a cab. This relationship would last 40 years on my part. It wasn't on hers, unfortunately, but I never forgot about her.

There was a lot more to this relationship. She was now managing rock bands and that's what she knew. I would see her sporadically over the next few years before she cut the ties alltogether. My only woman friend that I knew in my short life who was on her own — or so I thought. Maybe she had another man in her life.

A hard lesson learned.

Northlands Adrenaline

March, 1982

Going into Edmonton as the Oilers were in the midst of forming their dynasty was always a challenge. There seemed to be hall of farmers everywhere. Wayne Gretzky, Mark Messier, Kevin Lowe, Grant Fuhr, Jari Kurri, Paul Coffey and all the rest were a formidable foe. Throw in Calgary and the Alberta swing was a chilly and frosty trip.

Usually, NHL teams went out west to regroup and come together, but Edmonton and Calgary didn't offer that opportunity. Winnipeg, Vancouver and LA possibly were the stops on a good trip.

We usually arrived in the early afternoon, taking an early-morning flight the night after the Winnipeg game. Mark Pavelich was used to this weather, being from the Iron Range of Minnesota, so he only wore his light corduroy jacket with a toothbrush in his top pocket.

He didn't care if some players thought he was different. Maybe not crazy yet, but, oh how different. He could actually make money on this trip, for which I think the per diem was $34 a day. Both Pav and his roommate, Reijo Ruotsalainen, used to come home with wads of cash while I was constantly borrowing off of trainers Joe Murphy or Jerry Maloney. The captain has to look after everyone — financially included. Sure, guys brought money on the road, but after a few nights out clubbing, it disappeared fast — like pronto.

The winter western trip had three of the deadliest cities as far as cold temperatures went. With the wind in Chicago and Detroit nearby, there didn't seem to be any rest on the Western swing until LA. Then we could let our hair down, New York style.

On the western swings, we would be gone for 10 days to two weeks, since the circus was performing at the Garden. It was up to the veterans to show the rookies or younger players the ropes. Hopefully it wasn't the same places that I had to occupy during my rookie year.

Chicago Shirley (my mother's name), the sisters in Pittsburgh, the mole lady (Sandy) in Denver etc. All the cities had them and if you were a rookie, "Watch Out!"

We couldn't wait to get to the sun and fun of LA. With still games to go, there would be some hanging and banging before we entered California,

Most players enjoyed being on the road — unless you were on a bad losing streak. Then the smile came off your face pretty fast. The married guys wanted to party on the road and the single guys wanted to rest. That's what NY did to you.

In Edmonton, we had planned to meet up at *Barry T's*, the local hot spot, but those plans changed when my hotel room phone rang. On the other end was the sound of a sweet girl's voice. She said "Hi, Barry. This is JudyAnne McCarthy. Do you remember me?"

My heart skipped more than a beat. JudyAnne was the hottest girl in Langley Senior Secondary School when I was 16. All the guys wanted to date to her, not just my teammates on the Langley Lords of the BCJHL. She had an older boyfriend and was 'hands-off,' but looking was allowed … unless you got caught. She knew she was 'hot' in her own subtle way, which made her even more attractive.

"I read in the newspaper that you were in town, so I thought I would call and say hello."

Back then, there was only one well-known hotel, so we could be easy to track down. Even though I had more confidence than I had when I was 16, it was still JudyAnne!

I was nervous as all hell as we began the conversation. She told me she was living in Edmonton and would like to see me if there was a chance.

Oh, yeah! There was a good chance. I told her that I needed to meet my teammates for dinner, but she could come by *Barry T's* afterwards. I couldn't eat at dinner, as the anticipation was overwhelming. There were no cell phones or social media, so you had to actually engage yourself when you could.

Barry T's was crowded early. We had finished dinner and went out to the bar area. This way, you could try to be a little discreet. I was single, so it really didn't matter, but you're still with the team and always watch each other's backs.

I found a quieter area after buying a couple of rounds of shooters for the boys and kept my eye on the door. Through the maze of girls coming in I spotted JudyAnne. I recognized her right away. Wow! Just, 'wow' is all I thought. She looked just as she used to look in high school.

She looked around as I made my way towards her. When we met, I gave her a kiss on the cheek as we hugged. It was a great feeling. I was taught to be respectful, especially when it came to girls. Since the game was in two days, I thought, 'This is perfect! I get to party with my teammates and my high school crush at the same time.' I learned there's nothing ever perfect, although you might think it quite a few times.

We had a couple of drinks and became very close as we talked about our high school and present lives. She had been married out of high school and was now divorced with two young children. The babysitter was helping her tonight.

If you're with a girl, it's nobody's business but your own. You can be sure you'll hear about it the next day, so you try to silently disappear if possible. Some players spend time then go back to the hotel. Some stay later. Nobody gets left behind, girls or no girls. With JudyAnne it just seemed so natural and meant to be. So it was.

You don't want to go prancing through the lobby with a girl on your arm like it's New Year's Eve! You never know who'll be waiting. It's wrong, but players have done it. Me, included.

If you do, you'd better be the first star the next game or two.

Pav had his own style. He wasn't going to win any fashion awards, but he couldn't give a rat's ass about it. He just wanted to be left alone to create the magic he possessed as a hockey player. Darting in and out with speed and his own creativity.

Knowing where every player was on the ice, he would purposely act like he didn't see what was coming — then, at the last second, dart quickly to get out of trouble. He had magic in his hands, and his being small in stature at 5'8" was an asset for him in the beginning, He wasn't a player who played out on the perimeter, so going into the corners took its toll on him; it would any player but even moreso with Pav.

He'd go in full-speed to get the puck out to his wingers or defensemen. Ron Duguay became his go-to guy and Doogs profited quite a bit with Pav as his centerman. It really should have been Doogs going into the corners, which he did, but Pav was always there first — even with Doogs' great speed.

Pav had such a fluid, deceptive skating style, which always had him winning the races for any loose pucks. With defensemen getting bigger and more mobile, as well, it left Pav taking numerous high hits to the head area that were never called. He just toughed it out.

We arrived back to Northlands Coliseum after our pre-game meal and rest, ready to play the Oilers. The dressing rooms are fairly close to one another, so you will often see the opposing players stretching, kicking a soccer ball around, throwing a football, anything to get themselves loose and ready. We would do the same.

When you're getting dressed and the anticipation is building, every player acts in his own way. Some like to talk a lot or make jokes. Others are quiet and get focused. It doesn't really matter, as long as you win. Jump on a trampoline if you want. Just be ready when the puck drops.

We knew Edmonton always came out hard. They had so many top guns that we just wanted to limit them and keep them to the outside.

The first period was fairly even. It was fast, with hard, clean-hitting and creative plays. I was usually on the ice the same time as Gretzky, so we knew not to let him cut to the middle or set up behind our net. You had to beat him to those spots and take away his space. Easier said than done.

Shutting down the best player in the game was damn-near impossible, but limiting him by keeping 99 near the boards was your best option. It worked well until you'd see Kurri streaking down the wing with Gretz firing a tape-to- tape pass on his stick for a quick shot on goal.

At least they were shooting from the outside, where the goal percentages are lower. That was the plan, and it kept the game close.

Near the end of the second period, the score was 2-2 when Pav carried the puck into the Oilers end and was forced to the outside. He tried to cut to the net but instead curled into the corner. I was still at center ice but was reading the play as soon as he entered the Oilers' zone.

I beat the winger that was checking me and cruised into the slot and received a sweet pass from Pav and let loose a zinger, beating Grant Fuhr low to the stick side. My momentum carried me into the corner, where Pav was waiting, and I jumped into his arms like we'd won the Stanley Cup.

We were hugging, laughing and celebrating as our teammates came to join us. Fuck, it felt good. Sometimes when you get this kind of a chance, you don't want to let it go. We hugged and laughed extra long as Pav said, "Nice goal, Bubba!" I replied "Sweet pass Pav! I love it!!"

We laughed again before splitting apart and heading to the bench, where we were mobbed again. Usually, this would pump up the other team, but this goal had taken the wind right out of their sails. The second period was over, and we were now in the lead 3-2. It was a big goal and gave us confidence for the third period.

Pav had a lot of chances in the third and our defense shut down any offensive threats that came our way. Glen Sather, coach of the Oilers back then, pulled Grant Fuhr late in the game, but we managed to hold on for the win.

We all hugged each other and were elated with the win. When i came over to the bench, Joe (Murph) Murphy said to me "Bubba, stay out on the ice. You're first star and Pav is second!" When Pav came by, we hugged and laughed again. We heard our names announced, did a short skate and into the dressing room we went where everyone was all fired up,

Herb Brooks came in and told us what a great game everyone had played. When Herb said something, he meant it. There was no joking around with this one. I went over to Pav and said, "We got the green light to go out tonight!"

"*Barry T's*? he replied.

"Oh, yeah," I said. "Taxis will be outside"

I thought to myself, 'So will JudyAnne,' who I had gotten tickets for the game. She would meet me at *Barry T's*.

This was a big win all around. We shut down the Oilers, Pav and I were first and second star, then I have JudyAnne meeting us to party with the team!

YEEHA!! After partying awhile, JudyAnne then asked if I'd like to go back to her house.

I said "Let's Go!"

Once there, I greeted the babysitter, then said goodbye to her as JudyAnne's kids were asleep.

JudyAnne and I talked on her couch for an hour or so before heading into her bedroom. There were no cell phones.

I was up early and in my room around 6:00 am — still cutting it close, but having no roommate had its advantages. I packed up and went down for breakfast and mingled with the rest of the team. I got a hold of one of the local newspapers, which had a quote from Glenn Sather: "Beck was a dominant force last night and Pavelich owned the puck. We don't usually see that happen against us!"

I thought you better be first star every game when it feels like this! A consistent pro is what it's all about. I'd have to do it every game for us to win. So would the rest of the Rangers.

Life is a rollercoaster, so don't get too down on the low moments. There will be plenty of them — more failures than successes — so ride them out, then get back to living in the moment. The future isn't here, so no need to worry about it. Just live now. The moment is what you control. It's a great thought, so live it!

Big Bo

September, 1981

In 1981, the Rangers had their training camp in Sweden along with the Washington Capitals. The NHL likes to do this to promote the league.

We would play a round-robin with the Swedish Elite League. AIK was the favorite in the Swedish League. Bobby Hull came to our camp for a try-out. He was one of my childhood idols, so being around him was a fantasy come true.

While I was a rookie playing in Colorado and Bobby was with Winnipeg, he made one of his patented big rushes then came over the center red line and wound up to take a slap shot. Being the rookie that I was, I stuck my stick out to block the shot. The puck careened off my stick and went right for my throat at 90 miles an hour. It caught me right in the windpipe and down I went. I tried to catch my breath, but I couldn't breathe.

Our trainer, Jerry Maloney, came out on the ice and comforted me until I was able to breathe. At the same time Bobby Hull came over and tapped me on the ass with his stick and said, "Come on. You're a big kid now!"

When I heard those words, I got up and headed towards the bench, still trying to catch my breath. A lot of guys still didn't wear helmets — me being one of them — so getting a Bobby Hull slapshot in the throat instead of being hit between the eyes, I guess I considered myself lucky!

In Stockholm, we laughed about it as we went out for practice. I had loads of respect for Bobby, as I did for all the older pros, as they paved the way to give me the opportunity to play. Today's players should do the same. A special effort should be made by them to help build a facility to assist in the recovery of former players and their families.

The European ice is wider and longer with extra room behind the net, which defensemen love. All you need is that extra second to make a play and the breakout is quick.

⫶⫶⫶   THE CELL   ⫶⫶⫶

We would play all the teams included in the tournament. We would end up in the finals against AIK, the Swedish powerhouse.

Bobby Hull, at the age of 40, still tried his patented rushes, but you could see how age had caught up to him. We were looking at ourselves as it's inevitable when your skills will diminish. Some sooner than others. You'll know when it's your time. Right now, it was Bobby's time. The focus of the camp was on coach Herb Brooks and rookie phenom Reijo Ruotsalainen.

Reijo was a small Finnish player who could skate as fast backwards as he could forwards. He was so smooth it was like velvet watching him skate and play. He had all the skills and would play a big role in any success the Rangers would have.

In the final against AIK, we pretty much dominated them. There was something that was quite different about the crowd during the game. There was one section of the rink that kept chanting "F--- Off, Rangers!" Through the whole game. Now there were lots of children at the game, so it was hard to understand. They wouldn't stop until AIK scored, and that was only twice.

I finally asked Anders Hedberg on the bench, "Hey Anders, what's up with that section who keeps telling us to F--- off?"

He picked up his head and said, "Those are 'the Monkeys on the Mountain!' They are hardcore. AIK is known as the working-class city. It doesn't matter if it's hockey, football, golf or tennis: they want to be heard." In the third period, when we had a 6-2 lead, they got louder and louder, so we had a little fun with it. Some of us would go over to their section and tell them to 'F--- off' before the referees would come and defuse the situation but they only got louder. Whenever players had a chance in the last 10 minutes they would skate by, look at the crowd and yell 'F--- Off!' You didn't even have to say the words, just mimic them and it would send them into a frenzy. We found it to be quite entertaining.

When the final buzzer went, we all went over to our bench, where the extra players were that we had brought for training camp. We all hugged each other and enjoyed our first big win under coach Brooks. All the while the 'Monkeys on the Mountain' kept chanting away.

AIK received a second-place trophy and then they called me (being captain) out to receive the first-place trophy. When they gave it to me, I held it up in the air and spun around so everyone could see it. I held it up to the 'Monkeys on the Mountain' section and shook it at them. They chanted even louder!

Then had to put the trophy down as the tournament director presented me with a huge, oversized cheque for 100,000 kroners. I think it was around 1,000 a player, but it would just go into our slush fund that we would use at the bars in Stockholm. As I went by the bench, I passed the trophy to the next player, who then went around the rink, stopping at the 'Monkeys on the Mountain' section and shaking the trophy.

Big Bo

Our trainers said we had to hurry up, so I gave the trophy to the eight guys who weren't playing and they all went around running in their street shoes, shaking the trophy at every section. The "F--- Off Rangers" never stopped until we left the ice. We laughed all the way to the dressing room then drank Coke and Sprite out of the cup. It wasn't the Stanley Cup and we knew it, but it was a helluva good start.

We took the cup with us into the bars of Stockholm. We were the kings of the city — or so we thought. One shot of Bacardi was eight dollars US but we let it rip.

At one point, the Swedish actor Bo Swenson came over and introduced himself. He was already lit up and had been to the game. He was hugging us and ordering drinks. When he came back over we all started chanting "F--- Off Rangers! F--- Off Rangers!" Although we didn't like to hear it, we embraced it and were having fun.

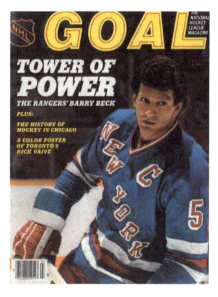

I started calling Bo "Buford" because that's what his name was in the movie "Walking Tall," in which he played the main character, sheriff Buford Pusser. It was another great revenge movie and was tops at the box office. Bo was getting along well with us when I said to him "Bo, go Buford on them!" He got this crazed look on his face. Just like Buford Pusser! He was now in character. He somehow got hold of a hockey stick behind the bar and shouted, "Nobody messes with Buford Pusser! I walk tall and carry a big stick!"

He swung the stick and knocked some drinks off the bar onto the floor and told the manager when he came over, "You might wanna pick those drinks up, sonny!" I knew it was time to go to the next bar.

When we got there Bo was already doing his thing. I said to Ron (Gresch) Greschner, "He's already going Buford!! Let's lose him!" There was nothing good going to happen now, so we got the guys together and went somewhere more private and enjoyed the fruits of our labor.

"We miss you Buford and it was great knowing you" as we walked the cobblestones of Stockholm.

Pav Comes to The Big Apple

September, 1981

Pav had been playing in Davos, Switzerland when scout Chuck Grillo from Minnesota, who was a close friend of Herb Brooks, talked Pav into coming to Broadway.

If you watched the 1980 Winter Olympics, the "Miracle On Ice," then you knew how good Pav was. I thought he was the catalyst behind the USA team winning the gold medal. Sure, it took everyone, but there were key moments in each game where Pav was involved. A lot of that team went on to have successful careers in the NHL -- some with the Rangers, like Rob McClanahan, Dave Silk, Bill Baker and Pav.

It was an odd relationship they had with Herb. Coaches have their plan to make the team win. If they don't, their job is on the line. It was a love/hate relationship with Herb, and I could tell right away from how distant the Olympic players were to him.

Herb was a master of the technical side of the game, but he seemed to carry this grudge around with him from being the last player cut from the 1960 USA Olympic team that went on to win the gold medal. That certainly would be tough, but he was an experienced, winning coach who now had to prove himself at the NHL level.

We watched the ascent of the USA team at Lake Placid and were shocked and amazed like everyone else. To have Herb and a core group of that team come and play for us was a blessing. The country needed that team to win, as Iran was holding US hostages at the time, and it brought the country together. America had been brought back to be the world powerhouse once again. That feeling of confidence is what a team needs to win the Stanley Cup and it was 1940 since the Rangers had last won. We would hear it often when we played out on Long Island against the Islanders, who had their own Hall of Famers and dynasty rolling.

THE CELL

Pav didn't talk a lot, but he was a tremendous, creative player. He could go North to South or East to West. Really, he went wherever the hell he wanted. He killed penalties, played the power play and was our best centerman.

Some players didn't take the time to get to know him. They missed out on his simplicity. The simplest part of a human being: the soul. Yes, to some he was an introverted outcast, but to others he was a cool cat. It's of no concern when they wear the same jersey as you.

Pav lived up in Rye, NY, near our practice facility and hung out with fellow rookie Reijo Ruotsalainen. Reijo didn't speak English very well, so we often wondered what they talked about. It was hard to get a word out of Pav at the best of times. Some would call them the "Odd Couple," but they were two of the top players on the team. When you see and feel the creativeness of the game, it's magic — and that's what Pav and 'Rexy' were: MAGIC!

Before Espo retired and Don Murdoch was traded, only Ron Duguay, Ron Greschner and myself lived in the city. All the others lived up near Rye and made the commute to the city for games.

If you took the time to get to know Pav you had to do it quick. If the conversation was about fishing or hunting, then you had his attention; anything else and you'd lose him. That's why a lot of players misunderstood him. He just loved to play hockey and didn't want to put up with any bullshit that came his way. No TV, no radio interviews — just play hockey, and that, he did very well.

When you were on the ice with him, you always tried to get into the open. In any zone, just find some space and he would get you the puck.

That's MAGIC. Sometimes I would call him Magic and he would say "Come on Bubba, leave it alone." No attention. Fly under the radar. Just play hockey. That was Pav.

Numerous times he'd go into the corners and take a beating getting the puck to Ron Duguay, who had his best seasons playing with Pav. He could usually weave his way through traffic, but along the boards, you'd pay a price. Since Pav was 5'8," it was his head that was absorbing most of the hits. Like most players in the 1980's, concussions were just headaches and you played through it. We had the best doctors and medical staff with the Rangers but everyone makes mistakes, but it was the league protocol.

When Pav was once diagnosed with a concussion, after he came back to play, he wasn't the same player. His timing was off and the tape-to-tape passes were now out-of-sync. His game desire was not the same.

Did he have a serious brain injury? You couldn't tell by talking with him; neither could the doctors. He was cleared to play, but who knows if he was ready to play. That was left up to the player. The magic was there sporadically, but to be a great pro, it's all about consistency.

Pav Comes to The Big Apple

In the early 80's, we got better every year. To get to the Cup, we had to go through the Islanders.

In the 80-81 season, we had toughness and skill and proved it by beating the LA Kings and St. Louis Blues, who both finished in the top three of the league. In the semis, we were ousted by the tough Islanders, who went on to win their second Cup.

In the 81-82 season, we finished second in the conference. In the first round, we beat the Flyers but were defeated by the Islanders in the conference finals and again they carried home Lord Stanley.

Through those years, we had some great players and leaders. Our rosters included Ron Duguay, Mike Rogers, Mark Pavelich, Ed Johnstone, Don Maloney, Dave Maloney, Reijo Ruotsalainen, Dave Silk, Robbie Ftorek, Mikko Leinonen, Pat Hickey, Mike Allison, Tom Laidlaw, Steve Vickers, Andre Dore, Rob McClanahan, Dean Talafous, Jere Gillis, Carol Vadnais, Ed Hospodar, Peter Wallin, Tom Younghans, Tim Bothwell, Steve Weeks, Mark Morrison, Mike Backman, Anders Hedberg, Lance Nethery, Cam Connor and Nick Fotiu. Our goalies were listed in the playoffs as Steve Weeks, Eddie Mio, Steve Baker, John Davidson and John Vanbiesbrouck.

This lineup was a strong combination of leaders, toughness and skill, but we were still finished off by the Islanders in six games.

This was getting to be a tough pill to swallow against our cross-town rivals. We needed to improve in every area to make a legitimate run for the Cup. From goalie on out, there would be changes at most positions. Herb wasn't happy, then it fell onto the captain's shoulders — which was me.

From May until September, through the hot, humid New York summer, all you heard was, "When are you guys going to beat the Islanders?!" My doorman and mailman even got into the action. The only good news was my air conditioning was on high to drown out any thoughts so I could get some sleep. Sometimes, I positioned myself right underneath the machine — which was fine until I got the first drip in my eye. Then the second and third came before I got up and put a bowl underneath it.

Through the summers, I trained like Herb had asked. His training manual was a book in itself, and by then I knew my body fairly well. A lot of players would try to make a trip home during the sweltering month of July, then come back in August to prepare once again for the grind of the season. By this time, I was in the weight room every day, then onto the bike to race through Central Park as part of my training regimen.

I worked out at the midtown YMCA on 47th Street. There were a lot of characters in there, including 'Joe,' who was the resident strongman in the weight room. He was a Giants fan, which usually meant you were a Rangers fan, a Yankees fan and a Knicks fan. On the other side of the coin, you were an Islanders fan, a Jets fan, a Mets fan and a Nets fan. That's the way life was in the Tri-State Area.

At one point, with Joe spotting me, I did two reps on the bench at 455 lbs. One rep wasn't official. With 225 pounds, I could pop off 28 reps and even hit 30. I don't think there was any other NHL player who was doing this kind of weight. I never heard or saw any steroids in the NHL. It just wasn't around yet. If I would have come across paths with it, I didn't need it — or I would have been playing for the Giants and not the Rangers.

I was really into my bike training and received an autographed picture from five-time Tour De France winner Bernard (the Badger) Hinault. My lawyer and good friend Rob Ingraham, used to help with the NBC-TV contract with the Tour and set up a meeting with Bernard and myself at his office. Rob kindly reminded me to bring an autographed stick with me. Bernard had already seen a Rangers game where we had previously met, so I came to Rob's office excited to see Bernard.

When I saw Bernard, we hugged and kissed three times as the French do, then Rob tried to help with the translation as the only French words I knew were from my Grade 8 Templeton High School class (which I tried my best to skip out of).

Also, my French-Canadian slang that I used in Montreal and Quebec City games wouldn't cut it. There was another man, Guy, who Rob had worked with doing the tour TV contract. Guy became the translator, as Bernard didn't speak much English. Bernard was more than a French hero, as he had thousands of fans, but loved coming to the Ranger games.

We had coffee, and then Bernard went into another room and came out with one of the bikes he had. He had it adjusted, as I was quite a bit taller than him. My expression was like a kid at Christmas as I hopped up into the saddle. Wow! Just sitting on it was an incredible honor. I jumped off after a minute or so and excused myself to go into the other office to get my autographed hockey stick. I was somewhat embarrassed as Bernard was letting me sit on one of his bikes that he had ridden in the Tour and all I had was my stick.

When I brought out the stick, a big smile came over Bernard's face. He jumped up and down a few times before wanting to find a ball to play with. Rob brought out a tennis ball and away he went, stickhandling around the office. Guy said 'Bernard thinks he got the better of the deal!' We shook hands and all laughed about it as both Bernard and Guy were headed to JFK to take the Concorde home.

I trained on my bike all summer. There was a lot of good riders through Central Park during those years, but when I would pass guys going up 'Agony Hill' in Harlem, which was part of Central Park, their eyes would bug out and they'd have to take a second glance at my bike.

Bernard had also given me some stickers that I put on my bike. I think that it made me ride faster and get up 'Agony Hill' quicker. 'Agony Hill' wasn't that big, but they called it agony because the kids from Harlem would hide in the bushes and throw rocks at the riders. That was their turf, so when you turned the corner and came to the bottom of the hill, it was an all-out sprint with your head down. You were so full of adrenaline that you didn't know if you got hit or not.

I loved my bike, but the next year I got into a terrible crash in Central Park racing another rider. It was a hot August day as we took turns passing each other through the course. We finally came to a long straight section covered with over-hanging tree branches. That caused quite a few shaded, dark patches. As I sprinted around the other rider, I hit a hidden bump in a shaded section and went flying off the front of my bars. The other rider was so close to me that he landed on top as we slid along the ground for what seemed like forever. I could feel the flesh being torn from my body as the extra weight of the rider on me didn't help.

We finally came to a stop. It was just a racing incident but my shoulder, back, hip and leg all had open wounds with gravel in them. The other rider was fine, as I cushioned his fall. We got up and my bike was unrideable — not that I could get on it, anyway. The other rider asked me if i needed help to get to the hospital, but I told him I was going to take a cab home. I took the front wheel off and limped to Central Park West, where I hailed a cab. I should have gone to Lenox Hill Hospital, as it was right there, but wanted the comfort of my own home.

I was single, so there was no one to help. I gingerly took off my one-piece riding suit, which was difficult enough, and tried to climb into the shower. When that shower hit my back, with all the skin torn off, it was excruciating pain. As I turned the water off, I could feel all the gravel and pebbles embedded in my back. That was where the biggest piece of skin had been torn away.

I tried to clean up my other areas, but they were painful, as well. I did my best to clean my wounds, then used an old remedy that my mother had given me on my birthday. When I opened it, I was surprised to find a tube of *Ozonal*. My mother, being a nurse, used it for us kids at home for any kind of cut or abrasion to fight off infection.

I took that tube of *Ozonal* and spread it all over my back and other areas. My back felt like it was on fire.

I laid down on my good side to try and sleep, but it was a sleepless night. In the morning, my back had gotten worse and had become quite swollen. This wasn't right.

I called a dental assistant I knew, Anne, and she immediately came over. She was shocked to see what state I was in. I said, "Can you help me clean up a bit, please?"

"You need to go to a hospital!" she replied.

"No. Just help me a little please?"

She reluctantly complied. She looked at my back and how swollen it was and said, "What kind of cream is this?"

"It's *Ozonal*," I said.

"Well, it's no good for this, because you have to clean the wound first!"

||| THE CELL |||

"Yes. I tried that, but it was too painful."

"Well, it's going to be a lot more painful when I try to wipe this crap off, because it's infected everywhere. You really need to go to the hospital!"

It was only my stupid pride which was stopping me.

"Just do your best, please," I pleaded with her.

"Okay. You're going to need some antibiotics, which I'll call my assistant to deliver. Let's go into the bathroom."

She started to wipe away the *Ozonal*, and through the pain, I could hear my mother's voice ringing in my ears: "This will work on anything!"

Anne worked on it like a bad burn. After an hour, her assistant came over with an alcohol-based solution that stung like crazy, along with some antibiotics she got from her office.

It was around a three-hour process to clean the wound, dress it, then get most of the gravel out. We were all exhausted. Anne said, "If it's not better by tomorrow, then get yourself to the hospital! And don't put any more of that *Ozonal* on!" as she and her assistant left.

Darned Americans don't know anything about *Ozonal*, I thought.

Worked for everything when I was kid.

I took those antibiotics until I forgot who I was. All I kept thinking about was all the young children at the Lenox Hill Burn Unit that I had visited before. They prepare you before you go into that ward. You'll see young kids fighting for their lives and you're never the same when you leave. It's a powerful, gut-wrenching moment. You use a lot of tissues by the time you finally get home.

"Screw this," I thought. "Heal up and quit feeling sorry for yourself!"

It took a week before a big scab had formed and I started feeling better. When it starts getting itchy, you know you're healing.

My local drugstore was only a half a block away on 46th Street between Second and Third. I walked in and asked the pharmacist "Do you have any *Ozonal*, please?" and I showed her the used tube I had with me. She looked at the tube and said, "Sure, we have *Ozonal*. I use it for my kids all the time."

I bought the *Ozonal* and brought it with me as I went to Anne's office on 57th Street.

I rang the buzzer and she let me in. She had a surprised look on her face. She said, "Well, you look at lot better than a week ago."

"Yes. I just wanted to thank you for helping me the last week. I feel much better now. I brought you a gift that I think will help you!"

I passed her the bag as she looked into it.

"*Ozonal*," she said, laughing. "Best gift anyone's ever given me! I'll make sure we keep in the office in case of any little mishaps."

I said, "Thanks, Anne!" as she buzzed me out.

||| Pav Comes to The Big Apple |||

I walked back on the busy midtown streets, thinking about training camp that would soon be upon us. I stopped back in the drugstore and asked the same pharmacist: "Can I have one more *Ozonal* please?" She smiled as I paid for it. I felt like skipping when I left the store. I think I actually did for a few steps before I hit the light at Second Avenue and made my way across to my residence on 46th Street.

Going up on the lift with my little tube of *Ozonal* felt so good. Thank you, Mom!

Bone Crackling

April, 1984

Pav had led the team in scoring the past three years, and by adding Pierre Larouche to the team, it gave us an added scoring weapon. Pierre was as natural a goal scorer as I'd ever seen — Mike Bossy-like. He had a nice bonus for $100,000 if he scored 50 goals that year. With three games left, he had 48. If he got 50, he would not only get the bonus but would become the first player in NHL history to score 50 goals with three different teams. He scored 50 with Pittsburgh, 50 with Montreal and we were confident he could score two goals in three games. Pierre (Pepe) was on fire, so we knew it could happen.

In the three games, everyone was trying to set him up. He hit posts, had great chances in-tight, in all alone a couple of times, but it wasn't meant to be.

We were all disappointed, but with the Islanders looming in a short series, we had to move on quickly. You ride the momentum. We would need it, playing the best team in the league the past four years.

This would be our best chance to win in a best-of-five series. We knew we had a good team and were confident going into the series.

The Islanders still had all their big stars and could play any style. They could play it tough or wide open. Whatever you wanted. Led by coach Al Arbour and GM/President Bill Torrey, they fine-tuned the Islanders every year. They had Bryan Trottier, Mike Bossy, Clark Gillies, John Tonelli, Denis Potvin, Bob Nystrom. Billy Smith in net. The other Islanders were all vying for their own spots in the Hall of Fame.

If we could win this series, we felt we had a good shot at the Cup — even with the Edmonton Oilers waiting in the wings. If we did, we'd have our own Hall of Fame players.

Herb's weaving, puck-possession style of play had changed the way the NHL game was played. Herb was adamant about not dumping the puck in but to pass it back to your defensemen and regroup your forwards to keep on the attack. Herb would get so pissed if you dumped the puck in. I loved his regrouping style of play.

I was a power player and needed to play physical and big for us to win. I was traded to the Rangers for five players and cash, so the Stanley Cup was the only element that would validate the trade. It doesn't take one player to win the Cup, but I was the captain and leader. You won't win the Cup with one player or one leader. You need everyone to play their role.

Everyone had to lead. Everyone had to play their very best. Then you need the hot goalie.

We had other players that were looking for their own identity, and a short series with the Islanders was our best chance.

Craig Patrick, Herb Brooks and all our scouts had put together our best team yet. We had to do it now.

We had Mark Pavelich, Pierre Larouche, Anders Hedberg, Don Maloney, Mike Rodgers, Ron Greschner, Tom Laidlaw, Reijo Ruotsalainen, Dave Maloney, Jan Erixon, Mark Osborne, Mikko Leinonen, Kent-Erik Andersson, Willie Huber, Nick Fotiu, Mike Allison, Peter Sundstrom, Glen Hanlon in goal.

We split the first two games on the Island because of the hot goaltending of Glen Hanlon, and won the first game at home. We were up two games to one, so if we won the next game, the series would be over. It was an exciting yet nervous time. Just one game and we would finally take the next step.

I think the score was 1-1 late in the first period. The puck was shot into our end, where I raced back and picked up the puck behind the net. My speed carried me into the corner. As I took a look up ice, I just saw a dark blue blur, so I knew there would be a collision. Instead of bracing myself and squaring up for the hit, I lowered my shoulder to put my own force into the collision. I wanted to lay him out just as much as he wanted to hit me. That 'he' was Pat Flatley.

Bam!! it was like linebacker and fullback colliding. Instantly, I felt and heard a bone crack in my shoulder. I was up against the boards now, trying to get back into the play. It was a clean hit, but I held my arm next to my body. It was physical pain like I'd never felt before. As I scrambled to get to our net to try and help, I fell to the ice. Brent Sutter picked up the puck and lofted it over Glen Hanlon for an Islanders goal to go ahead, 2 - 1.

I lay on the ice in agony before trainer Bob Williams came out and helped me off into our dressing room. I instantly knew the series was over for me. Dr. Norman Scott came and assessed me, then called for the ambulance. It wasn't my first time taking the ambulance from MSG to Lenox Hill Hospital. I knew this injury was serious, because of the amount of pain I was in. I had a high pain threshold, but this one was right at my edge and I just endured it until we got to the hospital.

Once there, they immediately got me in for x-rays. I took a seat outside the X-ray room, where co-team doctor Bart Nisonson came out and told me I had a broken bone in my AC joint, as well as a badly separated shoulder.

"You're going to need surgery, Bubba."

"Can it wait until the series is finished?" I asked.

"Yes, but right after the series, we need to do it!" he replied.

He fitted me for a sling. Since Dr. Scott had to rush back to the game, Dr. Nisonson got me situated into a hospital room where I would spend the night.

Before leaving, he received news that we had lost the game, 3-1, and the series would be going back to Long Island for the fifth and final game.

I sat on the bed, all busted up, wondering if we could win the final game. Either way, I was going to be there to watch and be with my teammates. I had a day to rest, but still couldn't move my arm.

The final game ended up being the most exciting game I ever watched. I stayed down in our dressing room, where they had set up a TV. Nick Fotiu and I tried to watch it, but we kept going out to the ice to watch the game as it was nerve-wracking waiting in the dressing room.

It was a back-and-forth game, with Don Maloney tying the game late in the third period on a controversial high stick goal. It was rendered a good goal that would send the game into overtime. We still had a chance as the team came in to rest and regroup.

You could feel not only the excitement but the confidence, as well. We all felt like it was time for us to win. I didn't care then that I was hurt. "Let's just win," I thought.

The overtime started just like the game had ended. it was wide open, with both teams having early chances to win. Mark Pavelich, Pierre Larouche and Ron Greschner all had great looks to win. Mike Bossy came down on a three-on-one and elected to shoot a shot that went off Glen Hanlon's pad and went wide. Back and forth the two teams went until Bob Brooke had a great chance to win it before Billy Smith made a great pad save.

The puck went down into our end, where Larry Patey tried to carry it out before tripping on a stick and falling along the boards. The puck was shot around our end, coming up the boards, where Ken Morrow was waiting in the right-wing circle. He took a quick slapshot that beat Glen Hanlon to the far corner and the game was over.

It was jubilation as all the Islanders came onto the ice to celebrate. It was a gut-wrenching, desolate feeling for our team. We had played hard, and even though you were proud to be a Ranger, it was an empty feeling knowing that we let this one slip away.

The pain crept back into my shoulder as I went out onto the ice to shake hands with many of the Islanders, including coach Al Arbour. It was a hockey ritual and a sign of respect. To me, it felt like death. How could you ever endure a loss as big as this?

||| **THE CELL** |||

It's all part of hockey — the ups and downs — but this one took all the strength from you.

The dressing room felt like a morgue, but there was this underlying feeling of hope that was still there. Tom Laidlaw, Ron Greschner. George McPhee and Dave and Don Maloney all had positive things to say, but this loss hurt a lot more than my shoulder.

The reality of the season being over felt like a train had just hit you. I still had the shoulder surgery coming up but the feeling of letting the Stanley Cup slip through your hands was a deep cut that only the warmth of being on a team could mend.

Ted, Pav and Rexi

May, 1986

Herb Brooks and Craig Patrick had left and I was trying to heal up. The following season I would play 10 games, then get hurt again. This was continuous throughout the year until we were swept by Philly, also in a short series. It's not good when the doorman at your apartment won't even open the door for you.

The Rangers had brought in a shoulder expert from Europe to examine me. He did all types of tests and afterwards said, "You know, your shoulder is not meant to take the pounding you've been giving it!"

"I'm a power player and have to play that way to be effective," I replied.

After a lengthy conversation, he suggested trying to play a different way. That wasn't going to work, as I was no dipsy-doodler. Physiotherapy was recommended.

The off-season was healing time for me. It never seemed to end. I knew I was frustrated but was still trying to fill the role of a leader.

The new season started with coach Ted Sator running the ship. It's a beginning that everyone looks forward to. Early on in the year, I once again separated my shoulder.

I couldn't understand, really. I should have healed up and had done the work I needed in the off-season. So for all of the year it continued to happen. Four left-shoulder separations in one year. Play 20 games and get hurt. Recover, play 10 games and get hurt.

Our team was playing well under Ted. With most coaches, there are always players that don't agree with the decisions being made. Players just want to be treated like men. You are paid professionals and are expected to live up to those expectations. Seems fair to me and I loved playing for the Rangers.

For me, sitting on the sidelines wasn't a career. That's where I would be most of the year. I knew how injured I was but continued to try and get back in the lineup. It was difficult, as Ted didn't want the injured players giving off any negativity to the regular lineup. I was never negative when it came to supporting the team. I didn't agree that injured players should be isolated, but I wasn't the coach!

When the playoffs started, the team called up affiliated players who would not only help the team through injuries but inject their enthusiasm from management on down.

It's an exciting time when you're playing. If not, you try to be positive and help the team any way you can. So, I became part of what was known as the "Black Aces," the players who practiced after the regular lineup. This group sticks together the same way the regular lineup does.

I was practicing, but my shoulder wasn't feeling good. You put that aside to try and get in the lineup. All the players who didn't play understand that and ride the wave of the team. You play a supportive role. That's what is expected of you.

I was never happy when I wasn't playing. It was taking its toll on me mentally.

We made it to the semifinals against the Montreal Canadiens. Not only do you play them, you play their history. I was hoping to get into the lineup and watched the first two games from the very top of the Forum. The Canadiens were tough and took a quick two-game lead as we headed back to New York.

I asked Ted for a meeting before our practice up at Rye while the team was preparing for Game Three. We discussed whether my shoulder was good enough to play. I, of course, said it was. Ted said he and the coaches had been watching me practice and that I could barely shoot the puck.

"I can still do a lot of other things, like just be on the ice," I said. Ted replied, "I'll talk it over with Dr. Scott and we'll see before the game."

YEAAAAAAAAA!! This was my chance. I prepared the next day like I was going to play. Went into the dressing room early, fixed my sticks and made sure my skates were good to go. I was fully expecting to play. It may have been wishful thinking on my part, but I was ready as I was ever going to be.

Trainer Bob Williams came by my stall and said, "Bubba, you're not dressing tonight!"

I let out a loud "F---!"

Okay, maybe Ted didn't want me to break up the lineup. I kind of understood that. I also wasn't 100%, and that could have been a concern of his. I agree.

If you have a guy who's been your captain and leader and doing his best to get into the lineup, year-in and year-out, when the past five years he's given everything he's had mentally and physically, do you take that chance? For me it was a yes! Maybe I could inject some much-needed adrenaline into the team. That would be at the cost of another player sitting out.

I slowly took my gear off and was resigned to the fact that this was it.

At that very time, Dr. Scott came into the dressing room, and I said, "Hey, Doc, can I talk with you?"

"Sure, Bubba. Let's go into the back."

There we found an empty room, like he knew what I was going to ask him.

"Did Ted ask you if I could play tonight?"

"No. I've seen him a couple of times already and he didn't say anything."

Now I started to get angry. I walked out of the room and changed into my clothes. Ted didn't want me at the game, so I went home and watched the game on TV.

We got knocked out in five games. Our season was over, and we would have a year-end party in the parking lot of Rye Playland. I went to the party and the players talked about the season. Some were elated that we made it this far. For me, it was the Cup or nothing.

I was still mad about my own situation. My shoulder injuries didn't help but it was now principle for me.

Pav, Rexi and myself would all leave the team the next season. Ted went and knocked on Pav's apartment door, got no answer. Rexi wanted to go back to Finland and play. For me, it was the fact that Ted said he would talk with Dr, Scott and after I discussed it with Dr. Scott, Ted had not even brought it to his attention.

That was enough for me. When your coach doesn't believe in you, then how can you play for him? Why would three of your top players all want to leave?

A couple of weeks later, I announced my retirement. It was the biggest loss I had to endure, especially having to retire injured.

When I say "BIG," it hurt. The Rangers had traded five players for me, and the only way the trade would be validated was for us to win the Cup, with me playing a large part in that. I fell into alarge black hole.

Both Pav and Rexi moved on. Pav loved hockey and he just wasn't having fun anymore. Rexi most likely the same. We had our run and didn't get there. The three of us would all come back to play in the NHL.

While I was back in Vancouver, Glen Sather called me to come and play for Edmonton. My shoulder was still giving me problems, so I wasn't comfortable making any decisions. So Glen called Rexi, who was playing in Finland. Rexi said yes, and would come back and win his Cup in Edmonton.

Pav went back to Minnesota just to be free. Nature was always therapy for him and he needed a good dose of it. After some time, Pav made his decision to come back. It could be money or just that chance to play on a team that you had done all your life.

During my time in Vancouver, I started to play hockey with the local East End hockey team known as the Rockets. Big R, Freddie D, Danny the Kid, Silas McKinney, Louie and Johnny D, Joe Scorta. All of them big personalities. We played on Sunday nights and the theme was, if you were with a girl on Saturday night then you had to wear her panties to the game on Sunday.

THE CELL

"Sunday is Panty Day!" After a while it was just wear panties. We'd sing songs in the showers afterwards. For non-contact games, there was a lot of shredding going on in the corners!

I was now having physiotherapy sessions with local guru Alex McKechnie. Alex had been flying down to LA to work with Shaquille O'Neal and the Lakers, and was known as one of the best in the business. After continuing to work with him, my left shoulder and the rest of my body started to feel strong again. Many of the Vancouver Canucks used to come to him, so the word got out that I was training with Alex.

Vancouver Canuck Stan Smyl was also a great friend. Stan and I went back a long way and nothing would ever change that.

First, Pat Quinn called and asked me a number of questions on how I was feeling. That in turn would lead to an interview at his house in the British Properties, an affluent part of West Vancouver.

Pat was well-respected, and I was excited to be meeting him. Pat's wife answered the door and led me into the living room. Pat came out a minute later and we sat down and started in on how I was feeling.

"Alex says you're strong as a bull!" Pat said.

"I'm feeling a lot better now, Pat."

"Are you ready to play?" he asked.

"Yes. I think I'm ready now."

We talked a little further before I left. It was a short 20-minute drive home, but left me with a lot to think about. It was only complicated more when I turned into my driveway and thought I could hear my phone ringing inside my house.

I hurried in and answered the phone "Hello."

I listened to the voice on the other end.

"Hi, Bubba. it's Wayne Gretzky here. How would you like to come and play for the Kings?"

Wayne said, "We have a lot of veteran players and we'll think you'll fit right in."

I told Wayne that I had just driven back to my home from visiting Pat Quinn.

"(Owner) Bruce McNall would really like to see you with the Kings," Wayne said.

After a short discussion with Wayne, I told him I would get back to him ASAP.

I called my lawyer, Rob Ingraham, in New York and told him what had happened.

Growing up in Vancouver and following the Canucks, it seemed like a childhood dream to play for them. Rob mentioned that maybe playing in LA, I could slip under the radar, as there were so many veteran players already in the lineup. That is, if I could make the team.

I'd never thought like that wherever I tried out, but that's what the reality was. We decided to leave it up to the Rangers to make the deal. Three years off was a long time, and although it had been fun playing with the Rockets, I knew the pace was going to be quicker and I would need time to adjust.

The problem was, you don't have time when you're playing in the NHL.

The deal was made, so off to California it was.

LA had always been the place where older players go and retire. Live on the beach and play your career out. Not with Gretz there and all the other veteran players. There was a different mindset, and that was to win the Cup. That's what we were focused on, but you could have some fun while doing it.

Life on the Strand at Hermosa Beach was great. I loved the beach, and Marty McSorley lived just up the Strand in Manhattan Beach, so we became good buddies. He asked me one day, "Hey Bubba, do you want to throw the baseball around?"

"Yeah, sure, Marty," I said.

He went back to his place while I waited on the Strand. He came back with a couple of baseball gloves and a hardball.

We went out on to a secluded part of the beach and began to throw the ball. We were just in our shorts with no shoes, so there wasn't a lot of protection. Marty began throwing the ball faster and faster. He threw it low and high. A couple of them were right at my toes!

I said, "Marty, can you slow it down a little, please?"

"Sure, Bubba. No problem," he replied.

Now, I played lots of baseball growing up, and had seen fastball pitchers when I was at bat, but that was a few years back, playing Babe Ruth at Clinton Park. Marty was starting to throw as hard as he could, and I was doing the same.

I said, "Marty we better slow down or someone's going to get hurt!" — meaning we were going to throw our arms out.

He just smiled and continued to throw fastballs until I took a 90 mph one right in the palm of my hand.

"Okay that's it!" I said. Damn, my hand was hurting and my throwing shoulder seemed all out of whack.

He came over with a big smile on his face and said, 'Let me know when you want to practice some more!"

"Oh, I'll let you know all right!"

I couldn't feel my left hand and my right arm felt like it was falling off. "Let's go to the pier and eat," I said. We used to hang out there a lot. Great bars with good food and always entertaining.

If you went to one of our practices, you wouldn't be able to recognize Wayne Gretzky. He always worked hard, but just made himself fit in with the rest of the team. During the games, he would turn it up to another level that was unbelievable to be part of and to watch. He was a master at turning up the dial.

||| THE CELL |||

During practice, all the defensemen wanted to take him on during any one-on-one drills. You wanted to see how really good he was. Wayne knew it and would have fun.

He always tried hard but you would get pissed off if you didn't see the real Wayne.

You would just laugh about it the same way he did. Games were different. I had played against him when I was with the Rangers. We always tried to keep him to the outside and never let him set up house behind the net. He was the best at reading defenses and waiting for other players to join the play. He was the best at everything and super-competitive. He really was Wayne Gretzky.

So was the Forum Club inside the Forum, where the Kings played.

After the games, the players would go up and meet their wives or girlfriends. There was always a large curtain drawn across to separate the crowd at the circular bar from the players.

I had a beautiful girlfriend in Vancouver and had no intentions to get involved with anyone. I thought I'd have a quick look, so when everyone began to leave and I had driven to the game by myself I thought, "Okay." I went outside the curtain and there seemed to be a party everywhere.

I tried to find a place at the bar and found a small opening. It was next to a couple of tall girls. I ordered a drink, and within a couple of minutes began a conversation with them.

"How did you enjoy the game?" I asked both of them.

One of them replied, "I thought we were going to the Lakers game."

We all laughed and started into the conversation. They were identical twins and hot as could be. I was faithful to my girlfriend, but I could not get over how hot these girls were. I thought to myself, "This is what LA is all about! Beautiful women and living on the beach!" You had to think hockey first or everything else wouldn't be any good!

It wasn't easy. My girlfriend was back in Vancouver, looking after my dog and waiting for me. I could never hold down a relationship and this was proving my point.

They became great basketball fans and I became fans of theirs!!

I knew my timing was a little off and a step slow during the games. I thought I was improving with each practice and game. Being off three years was difficult. Timing is so important. It affects your creativity and confidence.

The coaching staff came to me and said they were going to go with a different lineup. I would only play if someone was injured or if they decided to throw me into the lineup.

I'd felt this feeling before in New York. It wasn't good. You work hard at practice, train before and after, then try to be a positive influence around the team.

The trading deadline was coming up. I thought that I had put in all this hard work the past three years to have the chance to play. Now, I was just watching. Nothing is good enough when you're not playing.

I'd already been through this in New York. The circumstances were different but the result was the same: Sit and watch.

I called GM Rogie Vachon and asked to meet with him. During the meeting, we discussed my situation. I asked him if it was possible to trade me. There wasn't a lot of time before the trading deadline. He told me he would try and work on it.

The trading deadline came and passed and no deal was made. Rogie came to practice and I met with him afterwards. The conversation was brief.

A couple of days later I was getting dressed for practice. Coach Tom Webster yelled at me in front of the other players getting dressed, "Bubba, take your stuff off!"

That was it. My comeback was over. No handshake, nothing.

I left practice quickly and went home. I called Rob in New York and told him what happened. I always called him when something went wrong.

Coming to terms with another retirement was difficult. Hard to accept. Trainer Pete Demers called me and asked if I was okay. Pete had become a good friend to me. Marty also called, checking on me.

The drive back to Vancouver was a long and lonely one. I thought about my career and had I become such a bad guy that you couldn't even shake hands with?

"Screw them," I thought. "No respect!" Such a simple thing but means everything! I guess it had to be me requesting the trade.

I knew the Rockets would welcome me back!

Mark

March, 1984

I hadn't been thinking of Mark, hadn't seen anything on TV about him. He wasn't in my mind in any way. I had seen him at a Ranger function in New York a few years back, where he gave me the same hug and laugh as when I scored that goal in Edmonton. He wrapped his arms around me as I did him. It took me back in time and felt oh, so good.

"Bubba, how you doing?" As he wrapped his arms around me and laughed.

"Pav, my man, you're still setting me up!" We laughed and grabbed a couple of beers.

We talked a little, but as always, he was very discreet on any subject you want to discuss. You will get the general conversation from him, and then he will lean in and talk very close so only you and he can hear. Mostly, only he can hear.

Mark was such a kind, gentle soul that you had to love his individualism. Still, some guys didn't. Even after retiring, not a lot of former players gave him the time of day. I understand that players have their own little cliques and are uncomfortable when someone tries to enter their circle, but it's a team, man! Everyone is accepted, goal scorer or not. You understand that everyone's days are numbered but we had to win now.

That's what New York is. The pressure is always to win. There is nothing else. You feel it every day, and not only deal with it but embrace the pressure. That's what New Yorkers do. Deal with the pressure.

Pav didn't care one way or the other. I guess that's why I loved him.

He was a gentle man — not only a creative player but artistic in his guitar playing. We talked some more during the evening. He told me he had some land back in Minnesota and would probably end up selling some. He didn't like anyone infringing on his territory, but the lure of money was always there.

||| THE CELL |||

It's always great when the Rangers recognize former players. There are some great players that wore the Ranger uniform and Pav was one of them. The Alumni puts their stamp on it and the players coming up will hopefully see the struggle that it takes to win. The losses come along with it. That's what you learn.

The struggle to win and the reality of losing. There's only two teams playing, so players throughout the league experience both. Everyone handles it differently.

You play in a full-contact league and know the rules going in. In fact, you like them.

I've played full-contact sports ever since I was a kid. Same as the rest of the players. You either looked for the contact or tried to get away from it.

In the NHL, there is no getting away from it once you go inside the perimeter. You're going to get hit, and that meant hits to the head. I used to give them out and didn't fully realize the prolonged damage they could do. There was no class on it.

It was the same in football: no classes but even more hits to the head. Two men running 30 mph and colliding head-to-head. All you have to do is watch videos of Dick Butkus and you'll see men get hurt. He was a great competitor but mean as all hell when on the field.

In hockey, you can skate faster than you can run. That equals big collisions. Even when you're dishing it out, your brain still rattles around. That's where you hear the term, "I'm going to rattle his cage!" You hit to hurt — not purposely, but that is your mindset. It wasn't just me, but it was the mentality throughout the league.

Pav took a lot of hits to the head. He was along the boards chasing the puck at high speed. That's what he knew from a young age. It's why he was the player he became: Relentless on the puck and always chasing.

When you play with that concept inside the perimeter, you're going to sustain hits to the head. Pav was only 5'8". Opposing defensemen are usually 6 feet and up. They play defense that relates to protection. Yes, Bobby Orr changed the way defensemen played, but even he knew how to protect the defensive zone. His skating was so superior that he could protect any zone.

Pav dug the puck out of the corners for Ron Duguay as they both had their best seasons together. Pav wore a helmet and Doogs didn't.

Going into the corners or playing along the boards, you're going to get hit unless you're Wayne Gretzky! Helmet or no helmet, your brain still moves around when you get hit. It's not good, and in Pav's case it really cost him his career. He sustained a lot of hits to the head. Almost every player does, but with Pav, it was more often.

When you're playing on a team, you see each other every day. You notice mood swings, but that happens through the season. That's the pressure of winning.

Pav was hit with a body check to the head. He came off the ice a little squirrelly and didn't play the rest of the game. The official status was a concussion. I think he had probably a few more before then. It was so hard to tell because you played, hurt or not.

||| Mark |||

When you're the captain of the team, part of your job description is to protect your teammates. It should be everyone's responsibility, but the captain feels it more. When Pav came back and played, I noticed he wasn't the same freewheeling player as before. He was more controlled, and that took away his confidence as the player he was: Freewheeling, creative, fun to watch and great to play with. It was like when you were growing up. That was the game you knew, thanks to the players that came before you.

To me, after that concussion, he was never the same.

The Dream

April, 1991

It was years later when I had the dream. I was living and working in Hong Kong.

It was very vivid.

Pav and I were riding horses on a ranch. He was on a little paint and I was on a big chestnut. We had stopped to give the horses a rest, and there was a big pasture ahead of us.

Pav said "Come on, Bubba. Lets go!"

"No, Pav. We have to wait for the rest of the guys to come," I replied.

All of a sudden, he just took off. I could hear him urging his horse on.

He was in a full-out run as I took off after him across the pasture.

My horse was bigger and had a longer stride. Just as I was about to catch him, he pulled his horse up and I went flying by him. I could hear him laughing. The same laugh when he set me up in Edmonton for the goal I scored. The same laugh when I met him at the Ranger event in New York. That was the dream.

It was the only dream I ever had of Pav. I wasn't thinking of him beforehand or in any recent times. I remember that when I woke up, I tried to get back to sleep quickly to get back in the dream, but I couldn't.

Work was hectic at the time, so I had forgotten about it. About three months later, I was scrolling down my news feed on Facebook and I came across the article from the Minneapolis Star Tribune that Pav had been arrested for assault.

I read the article five or six times in disbelief. I then thought, how I could reach out to any of his family members on Facebook?

I found Jean Pavelich and looked at her Facebook friends. Some I knew, so I thought it must be his sister. I sent her a message and she responded. She told me that Mark was being held in the county jail. She was afraid, and so was I.

THE CELL

Jean was just trying to get more info. She was looking after her mother and trying to see Mark at the same time.

"Has the NHL, the New York Rangers or USA Hockey called you?" I asked.

"No, I haven't heard from anyone," she replied.

I thought those three entities should be the first to call, even before me. They all must know.

Jean and I stayed in contact closely. I felt it was my responsibility to support her and find out what happened. Pav was a former teammate and friend.

During our conversations I told Jean that I had a dream with Mark and I riding horses at a ranch. It seemed so real now.

Mark was being held at the county jail. I only knew what was in the article and the info Jean was telling me. I knew being confined in jail was no place for a free bird like Pav, but the article said there was an assault that took place against Jim Miller. Jim was a neighbor of Pav's.

The article also explained that Pav thought Jim put something in his beer while the two were out fishing. Once back in from fishing, Pav pulled out a lead pipe and beat Jim with it, causing considerable damage.

This wasn't the Pav I knew. Who knows what happens over the years when you're not in touch with people?

I tried to get more info from Jean but she had a lot to deal with at the time. Trying to be there for her family, mother and Mark seemed too much to bear.

Mark was a local hero. I called Jean every day to try and support her. Every day, I'd try to get more info, but Pav was being uncooperative with the authorities. I learned from Jean that Pav was being moved to a psychiatric facility for evaluation.

A further article in the Star Tribune confirmed this. Having not seen Pav since the last Ranger event we attended, I was more than worried about him.

Over the course of Pav being moved, Jean began to open up somewhat about Pav's recent behavior — that over the past five years, she noticed Pav had been acting erratically. She was trying to do the sisterly thing and protect him.

More articles in other news outlets were coming out now. This was how I found out that Pav's wife had been killed in a home accident. After an investigation it was determined that she fell off the back deck of their house while searching for better cell phone coverage while on her phone. Pav was asleep in the house, according to reports.

This could explain his behavior, or could it be from other trauma occurred during his life? The hits to the head while playing hockey can also add up over the years. Was it CTE?

Pav being uncooperative wasn't helping.

The Dream

Being sent to the psychiatric facility didn't make much sense to Jean and me. An alternative site would have possibly calmed him down and maybe opened him up. This wasn't going to happen with the assault charge against him.

I continued to talk with Jean and over this time, no one from NHL, the Rangers or USA Hockey had contacted her. Why hadn't anyone contacted her?

Jean was dismayed at this point, while I thought it was outrageous!! She had too much on her plate to think about them. It's supposed to be the other way around. They're the ones that are supposed to think about you!!

It was about three weeks before I finally got to talk with Pav on a communal phone at the facility. When he finally came to the phone and said 'Hello," it was like the same old Pav.

"Are you ok Pav? I asked.

"Yeah, I'm okay, Bubba." he replied.

I tried to just have a calm conversation with him. As we continued the conversation, he told me we were being recorded. I didn't have anything that I was worried about being recorded. Maybe this was for security purposes. Pav would confirm that.

The first few conversations were very simple, as I tried to call every day in the beginning. I wanted to let him know he wasn't alone, and that Jean and I were going to help him.

In the beginning he thought Jean was against him and one of the reasons why he was in the psychiatric facility. I don't think he could process everything that had happened. People who were trying to help him he thought now were against him.

I was just trying to be a friend, talk with him every day and let him know he was loved. Most of all was that I was there to protect him. Like we were teammates again and that would never change. Living so far away in Hong Kong with the pandemic in full swing was challenging.

I talked to Pav about the dream I had with us riding at a ranch. He thought that was cool.

"Yeah, let's find a ranch where we can help people!" he said during one call. Even though he was in the facility, he still wanted to help people.

On most calls, I would start by saying, "How's the cuckoo's nest today?"

Pav would let down this low laugh as not to forget that we were being recorded. I was only trying to lighten the mood.

On most calls he sounded like he was the same old Pav, and then there were other ones where he would put on a brave face.

I knew he was sick. I could feel it. And Jean's conversations told the story. He also had to face the assault and gun charges. This weighed heavily on him.

Jean and I talked often, just like I did with Pav. We thought the idea of a Ranch that could help hockey players was definitely something for us to pursue.

THE CELL

I started to get in touch with former players who could help move our dream forward.

Clint Malarchuk, formerly with the Sabres, and Tom Gorence of the Flyers were the only ones who said, "Yes. I will be in this for the long haul!" Jean and I are forever grateful to both of them. We would add family members and friends as we went along, but it was a struggle.

We were all committed and determined to see this through, but there was a lot of moving parts going on. The evaluation of Mark was taking time. He was not cooperating, so we needed help. He needed an ultimatum as to understand that he could spend the rest of his life in there or admit that he was sick and needed help to the evaluators and at his next court date.

By this time, help was on its way in the form of Glenn Healy and the Alumni Association. I don't know how many days it took, but I had talked with Glenn in a previous conversation if the Alumni Association could help Mark in any way. We both agreed that Mark had to cooperate.

Glenn had access to legal help, and this is what it was going to take, so the wheels began turning and the Association stepped up to the plate.

Pav was going to need legal help and Glenn had also hired someone to help with the Association and the status of former players who needed guidance.

Both Clint and Tom knew of the urgency to get Pav into a different facility. Clint had been through his own trials and tribulations with mental health, and they worked hard with Jean to try and get the "D" removed in Pav's case — which meant "Dangerous." If we could get that removed by the court, there was a chance to have Pav placed in a less-confined environment.

A legal team from Minneapolis was now hard at work on behalf of Pav. The Alumni was supporting. Clint was obsessed with getting Pav moved, as he knew how fragile Pav was. We all knew.

Tom Gorence was the brains behind *The Ranch* team. We just kept pushing. If you don't, nothing will happen.

My role was to just be a friend to Pav. Try and put a smile on his face.

He was in a lot of trouble, but he was sick!

We all started to learn about mental health. I was calling Pav from Hong Kong almost every day, so I was living it with him. I think we all were. We had to take care of ourselves, as well.

While all this was taking place, we came up with a name. We wanted a Ranch but there are a lot of Ranches out there. So we came up with *The Ranch Teammates for Life*. It all resonated with us.

I mentioned it to Pav.

"What do you think of the name *The Ranch: Teammates For Life?*"

"Yeah. I like the sound of it!" he said.

The Dream

So that's what we went with. We all believed that Pav would get out and it was starting to feel like that was going to happen.

'Do you want to get out, Pav?" I asked.

"I have to get out Bubba!" he said. "I have a plan if I can't get out."

"What kind of plan is that?" I asked.

"I don't want to say anything, but it will work. It has to work," he said, with urgency in his voice.

"We're working on getting you out of there. Everyone's been working hard, because we want to see you at *The Ranch!* You are the biggest part of *The Ranch!*"

"Oh, I'd love to be at *The Ranch*. We could have elephants, giraffes, bison and, of course, horses and dogs that could help with animal therapy all in nature's setting. This would be great!"

Yes, it would be great, but this was taking time. Another court date was due, and this was getting the "D" dangerous removed from his case. Jim Miller, who was the one Pav assaulted, was fighting the procedure. He would fight extensively to have Pav sell his home and move from the neighborhood so they didn't have to deal with him.

Court and More Court

July, 2021

Everyone was anxious before the court case — Pav included. It seemed every court date was the same for him. He always felt they were just going to shut the door and throw away the key. Everyone in *The Ranch* group was fighting for him. On the other side, you had Jim Miller fighting against him.

When the judge's decision came down that the "D" could be removed, it was a damned good, positive feeling. We seemed back on track to get Pav into a caring facility.

Clint, Jean, Tom, the Ranch group, the Legal Team and the Alumni Association had all played a part in this crucial step. Pav admitting he was sick and needed the proper care was instrumental in this victory, but everyone had a role and fulfilled it. Great teamwork!! But there was never any time to rest.

When news finally came back that he would possibly be moved into the caring hands of Melonie Butler, who ran a service for veterans that needed help with mental health issues, we were elated. So was Pav. This meant a certain amount of freedom, something Pav thrived on. I can't begin to tell you the non-stop hard work behind the scenes — especially from Clint, Jean and Tom and Jerry Jormakka from the Alumni Association.

Pav would be getting out in a couple of weeks. He could have his dogs with him and even go fishing. It felt like a new life for him, and Melonie Butler treated him like a son. Loved him and guided him. Whew, he always knew how great it was to be loved. Anyone can fall from the top of the mountain. It's a true test of a man's character if he can get up, recover and move forward with his life. Maybe even climb that mountain all over again, step by step.

Pav was now out and getting the help he needed. He was well on his way to running *The Ranch* just like in the dream — well, at least being there.

||| THE CELL |||

I thought of the dream a lot. Could it actually become a reality, with elephants and giraffes, the way Pav had foreseen it — to not only have players and now veterans but their families, all healing together using animal and nature therapy? What a Ranch that would be!

Brock Cameron Beck

November 30, 1999

Brock was born in Brantford, Ontario, Canada, November 30, 1999.

I thought it was going to be the happiest day of my life until I entered the birthing floor and heard the blood-curdling screams coming from the fathers — sorry, I mean the mothers, including Brock's mother, Kim.

Brantford was also the home of Wayne Gretzky. I hoped the tornado would please miss his house!

Kim and I met in Vancouver on a blind date. Since she was almost 100 percent deaf, it was difficult at first. Then, she taught me how to communicate with body language and what I call 'lip service.' That's another way of saying "F--- off!"

Kim had a strong personality, and if she didn't like anyone, watch out.

I worried about Brock, but she proved to be a loving mother. I guess a daughter only a mother and a few others could love.

This was the first time for us to be parents, so Kim's mother and stepfather Jack supported us while my family was on edge in Osoyoos, B.C.

Kim's water broke in the middle of the night, so off to the hospital we went. I thought I was prepared, but you had better be ready for anything to happen. As we finally got into a room, the nurses brought blankets and pillows in. Then they started to monitor Kim's contractions. After they left the room, Kim grabbed hold of my shirt, tearing a long strip off it.

THE CELL

"You did this to me!" Why the f--- did you do this? Oh, my back hurts!" she said.

I just rolled with it. Everyone else on the floor was screaming, so it began to feel somewhat normal.

"I need my epidural, quickly. F---, my back hurts." I went out into the hallway and a doctor came by.

"My girlfriend needs her epidural quickly, my friend, or she's going to tear this room apart — with me in it!"

"She has to be dilated so much before we give her the epidural." He said.

"Well, dilate her now please!" I exclaimed. I wasn't going back in there until I heard some comforting words.

Then I got them.

"Barry, did you find the doctor with my epidural?"

"Yes. He's coming soon."

Just then, Kim's mother came through the door — and not a moment too soon, as far as I was concerned.

With Donna there, Kim seemed to calm down. I felt like I was the one they should be looking at now!

I gave Kim and her mother some alone time while I sat out in a chair in the hallway. There seemed to be babies being born everywhere! At least that's your perception. Nurses would walk by and look at my torn shirt and laugh to themselves. I'm sure they must have seen it before.

I went back into the room and now there was a flurry of activity.

"It's time for your epidural now, Kim," one of the nurses said.

I was glad to hear that!

The nurses brought in all this gear, and then I saw the needle. It looked like it was three feet long. Around to Kim's back they went and inserted the needle.

"Ah, yes!" she said.

Everything was getting a little crazy as Kim's mother, Donna, laughed at me while consoling Kim.

"It won't be long now," Donna said. Kim seemed to also relax, although she had some cramping. It's an exciting time but also nerve-wracking, with all the screaming going on.

The time had come. Kim had dilated enough to have the baby. We didn't know if it was going to be a boy or girl; we just wanted a healthy baby. It crosses your mind, "What if your baby has problems while being born?" All the checkups beforehand were good, so it was 'full steam ahead.'

Into the operation room we went. I was now starting to feel a little queasy. Everything had caught up to me.

There were four nurses and I asked, "Is the doctor coming?"

"I am the doctor," one nurse replied.

She then asked me, "Are you okay? Because we're going to start now."

She didn't wait for me to reply.

"Come up and stand by Kim's head, please. You can coach her from here!"

It was happening fast now. While standing next to Kim's head, I could watch everything unfold in the glass cabinets situated perfectly in the room like a mirror. As Kim began to push, I could see the crown of Brock's head in the reflection on the cabinets. I thought there was something wrong.

I asked the doctor, "Is everything okay?"

"Yes. Now push, Kim! Come on and push!' the doctor said.

Then, in this moment at the top of the mountain looking over the valley, a baby came sliding out.

The doctor quickly grabbed me and asked, "Do you want to cut the umbilical cord?"

"Sure!" I said.

She guided me down where I first gazed at Brock. It's an overwhelming feeling as you feel reborn yourself. My hands were shaking as the doctor gave me the scissors.

"Okay, right here should do."

Brock was already crying, so I placed the scissors where the doctor guided me and began to cut. It felt like a thick rubber hose. I had to use both hands and some strength before I finally cut through. It was magical, even with the crying from Brock.

The nurses put a little hat on him, then some socks, and wrapped him in a blanket. Then they placed him in Kim's arms.

Kim's mother, Donna, came in and we all started crying. We had a new baby boy!

We had already decided on a name if it was a boy. Brock Cameron Beck

||| THE CELL |||

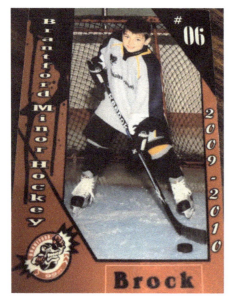

Back to Osoyoos, B.C.
February, 2003

After we got Kim and Brock an apartment, I flew back to Osoyoos to look after my mom and dad. It wasn't easy leaving both of them, but my family matters were pressing. My father Bruce's dementia was getting worse, and he was up all hours of the night. I would guide him back to bed, but who knew if he was going to burn the house down? This is what my brothers, Chris and Murray, had been handling with the care. It was now my turn.

At least, my father knew my name. We still had a window before the decision would be made to move him to Mariposa seniors residence, where they could provide full care. It was very close to us.

The decision was made, although my father wasn't very happy about it. My mother had long talks with him, but in the end, it was too hard for her— even with me there.

Once he was moved, my mother felt more at ease. She could continue to do the things she loved and still go visit my dad every day —as we all could.

I flew back out to Toronto, as I missed Brock dearly. I played with him every day and wouldn't let him out of my sight. He was a joy to be with and we had to put him on the bottle as he was tearing Kim's nipples up. When he was hungry, watch out! Kim couldn't take it anymore, so on the bottle he went. It made a big difference.

Kim and I talked about making the move out to B.C., where there would be more opportunities for us.

I had been waiting for an opportunity to get back into hockey, so my brother, Murray, and I took over the local hockey school in Osoyoos.

Osoyoos is a beautiful city situated in the Southern British Columbia desert, and was dry and smoking hot. It only had around 10,000 residents, but that swelled to

50,000 during the hot summers, as Lake Osoyoos was touted as the warmest lake in all of Canada.

Osoyoos was only 2km from the U.S. border, which was great for low-cost shopping and gas prices.

Eventually, Kim and Brock would make the move out to Osoyoos. We tried to live together at first, but that just didn't work. I would eventually find them their own place. The good news was that my mother fell in love with Brock — and he with her, the same way I had fallen in love with my mother.

We would take Brock up to the seniors home and he was now walking. He'd go visit everyone, even the old lady who was crying for her dolly. She scared Brock a bit, but when she came close to him and touched him, she would stop crying. She would say, "You're so beautiful — just like my dolly!" Then Brock would run back and grab me around the knees for comfort.

We would visit my dad and they both got a big kick out of seeing one another. Both my mom and dad loved Brock, as he was a little character full of love.

We would make Osoyoos our home, and even though Kim and I weren't together, we knew it was always best for Brock. I thought at least it was working, and Brock would soon be going to pre-kindergarten then the big step to kindergarten.

I was ready for his first day of kindergarten. I held his hand when we got out of the car, but he quickly took it back as he said, "I got this, dad." I walked him to the sidewalk and watched as he strolled to the front door.

Mrs. Sims, his kindergarten teacher, would be waiting for him in her classroom, as it was on the main floor. There were assistants to help show where the kids' rooms were.

I knew Mrs. Sims, as I was friendly with not only her husband but also her son, Kyle, who was a local hockey referee. Kyle and I would later become very good friends.

I was waiting for Brock after school. He wanted to do everything himself now. Open the car door, climb on up in. Yeah, he was a big boy now.

He loved to go up and see my good friend Wayne Pendergraft.

Wayne had a ranch with his wife, Wanda, and their two daughters, Miranda and Taylor. Both of them played tough hockey themselves and towered over Brock, but they sort of took him under their wing like a little brother. We would all become great friends.

Wayne got me helping with his pee wee team, which led to an opening with the local Junior B team led by Barry Dewar. Barry and I became friends and discussed me coaching the team. I'd never really coached before, but I thought i could handle it. Barry's son, Johnathan, would be an assistant, but we had our hands full from the get-go.

When picking the team, we wanted as many local kids as possible. This way, you can continue to develop through your minor hockey program. After a few exhibition games, we realized we'd have to go outside our boundaries to find players.

Brock loved to come watch the games, and I got him enrolled into the hockey program once he had learned to skate. He loved it but always wanted to play goalie. I told him "Once I played goalie for one game. We lost 7-13. I was good with a tennis ball up at the schoolyard, but the puck moves differently!" I told him.

"Come on dad. One *game*," he said.

"Okay, I'll talk with your coach, Dave Marcy, about one game."

It was the last game of the year, and if Brock's team won, the whole team would get free pizza from the sponsor. In the dressing room, I was helping Brock get dressed and telling him "Okay, don't do this and don't do that!" I was more nervous than he was.

After getting all his gear, he went to go out onto the ice and turned around and said, "Don't worry Dad. I got this." And out on to the ice he went.

I went up into the stands and tried to watch the game, but I was on pins and needles. Kim came to the game and so did my mother. Brock had his own little cheering section. Any time the puck came close I could see that the practicing with his friends Ocean and his brothers and sister had helped him.

Brock's team ended up winning the game and it was pizza for everyone. All his teammates came in and hugged him and that's what I think he really wanted.

When he came back to the house my mother gave him five dollars for the win.

"How much do I get when we lose, Nana?" he asked.

"Well, you can ask your father that one," she said.

I looked at Brock and I had been waiting for this. "Nothing —a big, fat nothing!" I chimed in.

Brock didn't like that, and he now knew he could make more money scoring goals and getting assists.

"Dad can you take me up to the 7/11 to get a Slurpee, please?"

Pizza and a slurpee — doesn't get much better than that.

"Sure buddy. Let's go!" I said. Now *this* was hockey!!

I learned quickly that I wasn't a very good hockey coach. Sure, I knew the game, but I took a lot of things for granted. I thought players at this level knew the little details of the game, but they don't. One or two might, but not the others. This is what I was supposed to teach, but these easy natural components of the game I thought all players knew — like, "Keep your head up!" If you get hit while looking the other way in a contact sport, it's like getting hit by a car. You'll feel sick for days.

There were good coaches in the minor hockey system — one being Jimmy Liebel. Others were Dave Marcy, Wayne Pendergraft, Igor Paulina and his wife Gabriella, Terry Dawson and Mike Harrison.

After a couple of years and not making a lot of headway, I stepped down from head coaching the team. Jimmy Liebel took over and slowly the players that we needed decided to come. That not only helped, but Jimmy was also a good coach. I learned a lot from him.

||| **THE CELL** |||

    Actually, I learned a lot from all the minor hockey coaches and formed friendships with them all. Those friendships usually took place at the Sage Pub, with owner Al running the show.

    I stayed on as an assistant coach for a while, then I slowly needed more time with my family. The team would eventually go on and win the Canadian Western Junior B Title. Jimmy had done a great job!!

Danny The Kid

October, 2006

Brock had now moved back east to the Toronto area, and I was missing him. Kim and I couldn't make our relationship work; any time that happened, she wanted to be near her mother. This was fucking hard — having them move back and forth.

If we hadn't had Brock, we most likely would not have had any relationship at all. The best thing I could do for Brock was to have a good relationship with his mother. Kim wasn't a social person, so I always worried for Brock. My whole family did.

My dad wasn't doing well at Mariposa and eventually passed away due to dementia. It was sad to see someone go through this disease — the brain dying and them not knowing who their own family is. Sad for such a strong man to go through and hard on my mother.

I stayed at the house with my mother, and when my brothers came, we discussed how the house was too much for her. It was getting close to time for her to think about moving to Mariposa.

It became a project for me and my brothers to fix up the house and for mom to start making plans for her next move. She also was at the point where she needed assistance — especially when I was not there.

My project was to build a rock wall out near the garage. My friend Wayne Pendergraft would help me collect the rock from the side of the highway. It was a damned hard project, but I got it done. For me it was all about giving back to my mother and father.

It was an emotional day when my mother put our house up for sale. My mother and father had come up from Vancouver to Osoyoos to retire. They became good friends with neighbors Ken and Karen Sieben, Bob and Sue and Naomi and Ted. Lots of friends came by to visit, as Osoyoos was so beautiful and inviting. We had many fantastic memories there. The people of Osoyoos had taken our family in as one of their own and we would be forever grateful. It had become our home, with Brock included.

I was out in the garage doing some work when the phone rang. I picked it up and Danny, the kid from the Rockets hockey team, was on the line.

He said, "Barry I just got back from a hockey tournament in Hong Kong, and there's a guy that wants to start a hockey academy there. I think you'd be great for it!"

Wow. I'd never been to Asia. I talked with Danny a little more, and he gave me an e-mail and phone number to call.

I grew up with a lot of Chinese kids, and went to primary and high school with them.

First thing I did when I hung up the phone with Danny was take out the map to try and find Hong Kong. It took me a while, as it is quite a way south. I was intrigued by it. I thought maybe this could be a new start for Kim, Brock and me.

It all moved fast, as I was first invited to Hong Kong by Mr. Alex Choi, on behalf of Mr. Thomas Wu, in January of 2007. When I landed in Hong Kong, it was 25 degrees Celsius (77 Fahrenheit). I'd just come from the snow in Osoyoos, and after the 13-hour flight, I was enjoying this. The discussions I had were positive. There was a vision, a plan and how to execute that plan. This was not only a great opportunity for myself but maybe this could work for Kim and Brock too!

When I got back to Osoyoos, it gave me a lot to think about. Could Kim and I improve our relationship enough with Brock included? I was willing to do anything.

I discussed this with my mom and brothers. My mom found a buyer for the house, so she would be moving up to the assisted-care apartments at Mariposa. My father had lived in the full care side of Mariposa.

There were major changes happening, so I thought this was a great opportunity for Kim, Brock and me. Kim and I talked about it several times. Hong Kong was an expensive city, so getting Brock in a good school was important. We would all just have to adapt.

It was all agreed that we would give this adventure a shot — together as a family. I loved the way it sounded.

But could it work?

It had to work!

Hong Kong, Here We Come

June, 2007

Once we landed, we stayed at the Panda Hotel in Tseung Wan until we got organized.

This was in late June of 2007, and it was hot. The Hong Kong summer was stifling. Having Brock with us was a blessing. I felt like a father.

We got him organized in a good school in Kennedy town, and he seemed to meet new friends. We would drop him off at his bus in central at 6:15 Monday to Friday and either Kim or I would pick him up.

Brock enjoyed his time in school, and both Kim and I were both heavily involved in his activities. We loved the school, but Kim became unhappy over time. Being hearing impaired, it didn't make things any easier with Hong Kong such a loud city. Kim couldn't hear and her hearing aids would give her feedback. This was uncomfortable.

There also are a lot of women in Hong Kong, and being hearing-impaired didn't help, as she could easily misconstrue sentences that were positive into negative thoughts.

For a western man, it seemed ideal — a pretty and adventurous place where we could get our feet planted. Kim didn't want any part of this. I thought it was working but Kim didn't.

She finally came to me and said, "I want to go home, Barry. It's not working for me. I'm going to take Brock with me."

"Why?" I asked. "He is organized and making new friends here."

"I don't care. I want to go home."

I put a lot into making this a family trip, but when Brock also told me he didn't like it, I thought there was some conspiracy going on. Brock was so happy, so Kim had to be telling him otherwise, because it wasn't me.

"You can leave Brock here and I'll look after him."

THE CELL

She agreed, but after talking with her mother after a couple of days, she realized that Brock is all she had. Without him, she had nothing. If she left with Brock, it would be I who had nothing.

After a week or so, we started to make arrangements for Brock and Kim to leave. I was going to stay because this was a huge opportunity for me. I had to work and pay money for my son and his mother.

I took Brock back to his school so he could say goodbye to his teachers and friends. It was a sad day for both of us. I knew he didn't want to go. We were having fun, but his mother was not. That was the straw that broke the camel's back. If she wasn't having fun, then it could turn everything upside down and that's what happened.

This was a big change that was for all of us, but with Kim unable to work, she felt there was nothing in Hong Kong for her — no matter how beautiful it was.

They would fly back to Toronto a short time later. This was just plain wrong. There was more to this than what she was telling me.

The fact was now we would be separated again, this time halfway around the world.

I don't think Kim thought a lot about this. She only wanted to go home and take Brock with her. This left a bad taste in my mouth. My company had gone to a lot of trouble to bring me in under the Quality Migrant Scheme for professionals that had to have stacks of supporting documents. She felt that nothing was for her, so said, "Fuck it! I'm leaving, and Brock is coming with me!"

So that was it. I would now become a long-distance dad. I was used to it back in Canada, but this was now halfway around the world.

Brock went to outdoor camp the first few summers but I wanted him with me. Kids can be persuaded to just stay in their area, and this is what was happening. I just rolled with it but wasn't happy about it. That time was for Brock and me, but going to a camp took up the whole summer and I had to pay for it.

One day he would get tired of these camps and realize there was a lot more fun for us in Hong Kong and Thailand, which was only a two-hour flight. So eventually that's what we did, and boy did he love it! Me, too!

Brock would always come at Christmastime, so we would go and help my friends Mike Raytek and Denis Gervais, who ran the Father Ray Foundation in Pattaya, Thailand.

If you've never been to Thailand you will never want to go anywhere else. From the culture to the kindness of the people, it's on another planet. Brock would help Denis at the Father Ray Christmas party and would help give out Christmas presents. This was better than any camp he could go to!

Until 2018, this is what we did. I spent as much time as we could but of course he was growing fast. I had asked him to come spend a year with me in Hong Kong after high school. That way, I could introduce him to people, help him learn the Cantonese language and absorb the culture and adventure. When I was back in Canada, we agreed this is the approach we would take. He loved it, so we started making preparations for his trip to Hong Kong.

I came back to Hong Kong in late May, but after many unanswered calls, I knew something was up. After talking with Kim, she told me, "Brock doesn't want to go to Hong Kong now."

"How the fuck could this happen? I just left him a month ago!" I was pissed now. "How could he change his mind in one month when we had agreed to him coming to Hong Kong?"

This scenario I knew all too well. "My mother found him a place in Nova Scotia, where he can study mental health and recovery."

"Did anyone at least ask me after we had all these plans made?" I asked.

"Brock agreed to it and this was a good direction for him." she said.

"But you didn't even talk about it with me. We already had plans made. He could go to school here in Hong Kong!"

At least Brock had found a direction, but it came with the cost of us being apart again.

Brock didn't say much about it, because he knew I was pissed, but at least he had found a direction in mental health and recovery. Lord only knows we certainly needed it in both our families. There was always a certain amount of pulling in each direction, but Kim and I agreed to always put Brock first.

So off to Yarmouth, Nova Scotia he went to begin his studies. He would live a few doors down from his grandparents, so he would have to check in every night. I knew they had a good eye on him. Between his studies and his girlfriends, it was hard to get a hold of him after that. I guess that's what University life brings. I felt isolated from him once again.

It brought an uneasy feeling upon me. The world was changing, and even though Brock was in Nova Scotia, I never felt at ease. The influence of the U.S. was never far away, and heavy rap seemed to be what most kids listened to. I thought it must be like the Beatles when I was growing up!

No, it wasn't like the Beatles. Now it was gangster!!

Summertime Blues

October, 2018

Brock came home in the summer of 2020. He had finished his first two years and graduated above all our expectations. He wanted to go back and upgrade his studies. I understood this and was happy for him. We all were.

He wanted to try and help his mother. I understood this.

I couldn't help but think that if he would have come to Hong Kong, we would have had the time of our lives. I knew I missed that chance to be with my son.

Brock said, 'I want to be the new Dr. Phil!"

I was proud of him finally having a direction. I was unaware that he was interested in mental health and recovery.

By now, Kim and I had put our differences aside and had a growing relationship. I think Brock and his new direction brought Kim and me closer together. I believe her boyfriend, John, of 14 years, was also a calming influence. He should have been given a gold medal, as far as I was concerned.

Being a "Long Distance Dad" wasn't my idea of a father, but it paid the bills and Brock seemed to have turned the corner.

We always had fun with our time together. It was only two or three times a year, so we made the most of it.

||| **THE CELL** |||

The Rangers had asked me to come in for the 90th anniversary event, so I asked Brock to fly in from Toronto. He agreed right away.

"You"re going to love it!' I said.

It was a great event put on by the Rangers, and Brock got to mix together with all the stars — Mark Messier, Brian Leetch, Adam Graves, Mike Richter and a lot of players that I was teammates with.

He met a lot of my friends that I hadn't seen in a long time and got to experience Madison Square Garden, the greatest arena of them all. We had a once-in-a-lifetime trip, thanks to the Rangers and the thoughtfulness of all the players. My friends played a role in his loving The Big Apple. After the trip, Brock told me, "Dad, I would love to live in this city!"

"Yeah. I know, my boy — you don't know the half of it!" I replied.

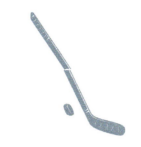

The Call

July 26, 2020

The years always go by fast the older you get. It was just another day home from work. It was summer and hot, so I thought I might go down to the pool. My phone had been ringing but I just wanted a quiet day. Finally I picked the phone up at 1:47 pm on July 26, 2020.

It was my brother, Chris. When he said, "Barry!" I knew by the tone of his voice that something had happened. I thought it may have been my mother.

Chris said, "I'm driving, so let me pull over."

He began crying as he pulled his truck to the shoulder of the highway.

I remember the words.

"Brock's gone. He was stabbed and he's gone." Chris was still crying.

"What do you mean, Chris, he's 'gone?' Don't tell me that!" I said.

"It's true, Barry. Brock is gone. Kim's been trying to call you but had to go to the hospital!"

I dropped my phone and put my head towards the ground.

"No. It's not right. You have the wrong info, Chris. Please call Kim again. Please?"

I was 12 hours ahead in Hong Kong, so there was plenty of time to get it right.

"It's true, Barry. Brock is gone!"

I was in shock, but recovered enough to pick up my phone and listen. I couldn't speak, I could only listen.

"The police are saying it was a road rage incident. They're investigating now."

"No Chris. It can't be. No!" I said over and over.

Chris just listened to me moan and groan as I lay on the floor.

"Barry," I heard him say, "Kim is trying to call you now. I'll phone you back after Kim calls. She's not doing very well."

THE CELL

Chis hung up so Kim's call could get through. As I waited, I moaned in agony. How could this be?

The phone rang and I could hear Kim crying through the speaker.

"Kim," I said.

She was just sobbing. There was no talking for a while.

"Our boy's gone!" I heard her say. "Brock is gone!" and she began to cry again.

We both cried into the phone because it was all that we could do.

Minutes flew by and the crying never stopped.

I finally said "It will be okay. I'll come as soon as I can."

I don't know why I said, "It will be okay."

From the time Chris had called me, I didn't believe it. I stayed on the phone with Kim and was now trying to ask her questions, but she was too distraught to answer any of them. She finally put me on the phone with her boyfriend, John Belack. John was calmer as now the emotions were changing.

"The police won't give me much details as they are still investigating. They don't want me interfering by knocking on doors. had already tried it once and the guy called the police on me!"

Your emotions can change quickly from, first, disbelief to, then, rage.

The news was already all over Canadian TV and radio, so it truly was real now. Brock was gone, but I would never believe it until I flew to Toronto and made my way to Binbrook, Ontario, 20 minutes from Hamilton.

My phone was ringing now from work and friends. You're in disbelief but then the hammer comes down and wakes you up.

I couldn't get a flight out for two days, but I could make up some time with the 12-hour difference. I went in and talked with my work and Cecilia Hon, our CEO, told me they would do everything to support me. Sam Wong, our Executive Director, reiterated her position. It felt good that the company, led by Thomas Wu, supported me. It was the first good emotion I felt.

I took a taxi back home, and then you're whacked by all these different emotions. It consumes you in the first 48 hours before you can even breathe. Just waiting for my flight would be difficult enough, and then there was the COVID restrictions. Whatever it was, I was going to make it to Toronto and then see how I would get to Binbrook.

All this time, while my colleagues Grace and Stanley were trying to put my itinerary together, you fall into a numbness state. You can't sleep, so you think a lot.

For me, it was the loss of my son. How could it be? How could it have happened when he had everything going for him? Who killed him? How many were there?

Rage and anger were quickly creeping in. I had to try and remain calm through all this, as I still had to get on the flight to Toronto and then make my way to Binbrook — which was a one-hour drive from Toronto.

The Call

Deep inside, I knew what I felt like doing —and that was to kill anyone involved. Just get there, I thought. That was my immediate goal. I had one day and a 15-hour flight to Toronto.

John had his hands full with Kim. Kim's mother and stepfather were on their way from Nova Scotia. John had a trailer in the back of his house that they could stay in.

There was only one other bedroom in the house. That was Brock's room.

At the Hong Kong airport, it was fairly straightforward. I had to fill in the forms provided by the *Arrive Canada* app. When I entered the Cathay Pacific flight, I noticed that it wasn't very busy. I think there were only four other people in business class.

I sat down and started to think about what was waiting for me on the other end.

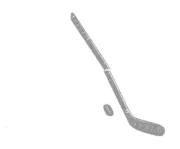

No One Here

July, 2020

The emotions you have run rampant. You just try to keep yourself together, because there's a lot more still to come. All the questions you have in your mind … It goes on forever. It's like an out-of-control plane that keeps spinning and you have to stop it somewhere. If you don't, it's going to crash — with you in it.

Staying calm, I could fall back on my leadership skills as being a former captain of the Rangers. That is what I tried to act like and carry that presence with me at all times.

I needed that strength and courage, including my faith, to ride this roller-coaster. Oh, I knew I would break at some point, but then it was time to get up and start again. So when I got off the plane from Hong Kong, that's what I was ready for.

I was the second one off the plane in Toronto. The first guy stood around, looking where to go. There were no cues or any representatives to meet us, so we just wandered around waiting for someone to meet us.

As the few passengers that were on the plane started coming off, I read an immigration sign so I began to follow it. Before I knew it, I was facing an immigration officer at his post. He looked at my document and said, "Put your document in the box down the line and proceed out."

It seemed all too easy. My bags came around the carousel and I took them off. I knew I needed a taxi, so I just went out the nearest doors. No one checked my bags, so it was the easiest customs/immigration I'd ever been through.

I opened the doors to go outside and there was no one there. It was like a ghost town or ghost airport. There weren't any vehicles around, let alone taxis.

I stood around and waited a few minutes. I felt a quarantine bus was going to pick me up at any time and take me to a hotel, but it never came.

||| THE CELL |||

A couple of minutes later, I saw a car coming towards me. He was dropping off a passenger.

I yelled at him "Hey, can I get a ride to Binbrook from you?"

"Sure. Hop in," he said.

Wow, I thought it was great to be back in Canada!

This is how you think. One minute trying to be positive and the next you're realizing why you're here.

As we drove out of the airport, I noticed the driver adjust his rear-view mirror. You notice a lot when your son has been killed. All your senses are heightened.

The driver said to me, "Are you Barry Beck?"

"Yes," I answered. I thought he might have been there to pick me up.

"I'm very sorry. I heard about your son on the news. My condolences to you and your family."

"Thank you," I replied.

This all seemed way too easy. We talked about what I knew of my son's murder, which wasn't much. He changed the conversation to the Toronto Maple Leafs, which even I knew in Hong Kong that they were struggling.

"Struggling" was a word I would become familiar with.

An hour later, we pulled onto Binbrook Road. looked around at everything and took it all in. Everything seemed to be in slow motion. I got out of the car and thanked the driver. He had made my trip quicker and easier.

Kim came out of the house crying and jumped in my arms. She kept saying, "Brock's gone, Barry. He's gone!"

We just cried in each other's arms. We didn't want to let go and deal with the reality, so we held on. For us, this was a different ball game now.

After a while, I said, "It's going to be okay. Don't worry, Kim."

"But Brock's gone. He's never coming back. Someone fucking stabbed him to death. I saw Brock at the hospital and had to identify him.

"It was sickening," she cried.

Donna, Kim's mother, came out and put her arms around us. We continued to cry some more.

John was out buying food. I'd never met John before. Kim always thought there was a lot of tension between us, but I never felt anything. I think we only talked on the phone once, so I didn't have any hard feelings towards him. Even if I did, this wasn't the time.

We had to become a strong team. We went inside the house and I looked around. I walked out into the back and met Kim's stepfather, Jack, and gave him a hug. He was legally blind but was still in good shape for 72 years old. I'd want to be on the same team with him.

No One Here

I could hear a car pull up in the driveway. It was John. We met at his car in the driveway and immediately hugged.

"I'm sorry Barry, Brock's gone," he said.

I told him, "Let's get the groceries in. It's hot out here!"

I helped with the groceries as Kim pulled my bag inside the door. We all started helping with getting dinner ready. Fresh, sweet corn on the cob and steak on the grill with small new potatoes with garlic. We all worked together.

At dinner, we had a chance to talk. We talked about where Brock was killed. It wasn't that far from the house. He was attending a small house party of 10 people, three of whom were adults. It seemed odd to me, but I had attended a lot of house parties when I was 16-20. There usually weren't any adults but the odd time there was. At that point in my life, I was chasing a hockey dream. I still went to parties and drank alcohol, but the world wasn't so divisive as it was now. It was like a time bomb and I think it possibly contributed to Brock's death.

We got dinner on the table, and I think we all leaned on one another for strength.

The two lead detectives would be coming over in the morning with any updates they had, and we had a lot of questions for them. We tried to have a family dinner as we all knew how difficult this road was. Our only son murdered. We didn't have any other children. There was an emptiness that had us in its grip. A loss that no one could understand — not even us.

At dinner, we talked of good memories of Brock and even laughed.

The laughing was therapy for us, and we needed it. The laughing was Brock. We could hear him as if he was having dinner with us. Yes, he was gone, but spiritually you could feel him. It was if we were waiting for him to walk through the door. He had a place at that dinner table and you couldn't help but feel him everywhere.

We finished dinner and helped clean up. We all went out to the trailer where Donna and Jack were staying. It was very quiet in Binbrook. We kept our voices down, as you could easily be heard. Binbrook Road was a busy thoroughfare and John's property backed onto 160 acres of cornfield, but this and every night you could hear a pin drop.

We talked about many things that night. Mostly, we talked about different theories of Brock's murder. The police had already released an image of a small white car, so we hoped that could lead to somewhere.

After a couple of hours, we decided to try and sleep. It had been a long day of travel for me, and everyone sleeps early in the country.

I was staying in Brock's room. Kim hadn't touched anything. I pulled my bag inside Brock's room and closed the door. I started slowly going through his cabinets. I felt like I was invading his privacy, but it was too late for that. The police had already done their search of the house before I came. It helped me to stay in Brock's room. I needed to be close to him. I could smell him on the blankets and I could feel him in the room.

I prayed that night before I tried to sleep. Prayed that he would have a safe journey. Prayed that there would be justice. Prayed for revenge. I looked forward to meeting the police in the morning.

It would be a sleepless night.

Hamilton Crime Unit

August, 2020

We were waiting in the living room for the police to come. It would be my first time meeting them. As they pulled in, Kim and John went out to welcome them. They came into the house and we introduced ourselves.

"Hi. I'm Detective Steve and this is my partner, Detective David.

"We're very sorry for your loss and we're here to help you. Please trust us. Right now, the interview process is still being done, but we do think Brock's murder was a result of a road rage incident. Unfortunately, because of the province of Ontario's restrictions on police, it can be frustrating for us."

I was just listening until I felt it was the right time to ask questions. "We could find the killers tomorrow or it could be months." Detective Steve said. "We have to be a team here.

"If we work together, it will help all of us. I've been working homicide for 25 years, and we just solved a cold case after 18 years."

"What about the white car you have on video?" John asked. "We've blocked out above the plate, as it could be an aftermarket piece that could give us a lead." Steve said.

"We have a lot of calls coming in, but we just can't tell you a lot right now." Steve said.

That didn't seem to help us right now.

Steve and David were very professional, and I could tell by their tone that they had been through this kind of trauma with other families. I trusted them, but we still wanted answers. That's all you're waiting for: answers.

Steve said, "Let us do the police work. If you start trying to be the police, then it could screw up our investigation."

"Okay, I'll trust you," I said.

THE CELL

Everyone else didn't answer. The police could feel our anger, but we wanted to cooperate as much as possible.

Steve said, "We'll try to update you as soon as possible. Again, we're very sorry for your loss and we'll do our best to solve Brock's murder."

We all said thank you and walked them out.

"We'll be back next week, or you can call us," Detective Steve said.

When we went back in the house, we started talking. We started going through Brock's friends, as he had only been back from Nova Scotia for a month.

He had a new girlfriend; could it have been a jealous ex-boyfriend? Was it like the cops said — a random act of road rage?

I was supposed to be in quarantine, but I'd had enough. I asked John if he could please drive me to the driveway and house where Brock was murdered.

We got into the car and casually drove by the house. The rage started to build. John had already talked with the cops a couple of times, but this was all fresh to me.

We drove by the house five or six times. I told John to stop the car. I got out and looked around, taking everything in. I listened to the wind and heard the birds singing.

I breathed in the air … slowly.

I tried to envision everything that happened. How my boy was murdered.

I said to John, "Let's go back to the house and talk."

Back at the house, we sat down at the table and put our own plan together. John had some contacts, and so did I. Others in the family had theirs. We weren't going to wait months to catch the murderer. We wanted him now! So we set the wheels in motion.

We needed hunters with their ears to the ground. My good friend of many years in New York, Marie Horn, helped us put a *GoFundMe* page together for a reward. We wanted people to feel part of the team that brought the murderers to justice.

Marie did a great job with the page, and we reached a limit that we thought could make a difference.

We had some meetings to get those hunters to find a name. That's all we wanted. Just a name.

During one meeting, we took all our phones and put them in the other room. Then we talked. Everyone knew Brock, so we wanted this guy bad.

Everyone at the table was ready to go to war. After everyone left, I told John I was going for a run. I needed to know more about this neighborhood.

I would run down to the main intersection of Binbrook Road and Highway 57. If this is where the cars first met in the road rage incident, why did they have such bad images of the car? The main intersection should have high-quality cameras. This didn't make sense to me.

I kept running down Binbrook and came to the house where Brock was murdered. I was hoping to see the owner outside but instead saw the neighbor watering her lawn.

She was very friendly when I told her my story. She offered her condolences. Then I asked if we could go into her back yard and talk. She happily agreed.

She said, "My husband is still at work. Do you want to wait for him?"

"Sure, we can wait for him."

I just got into general conversation with her. Then I started asking her questions.

Did you hear anything that night?" I asked.

"No, not a thing — and we had all of our windows open," she said. "I found out recently that there was more than two guys in the car. maybe three or four."

"Oh. I didn't know that."

I found that odd. It happened at 1:30 in the morning, so maybe they had gone to bed. With two small children, maybe this could be true.

About 20 minutes later, the husband came home. His story matched his wife's. I was starting to make some headway, forming the outside of the puzzle until I could fill in the middle.

There would be more people that I would need to talk to.

Brock's girlfriend was one. I messaged her and asked to meet her for lunch. She was living with her grandparents after some family problems.

She only lived a few doors down from Brock, so I asked her out to lunch. I was good at reading people, so if she was hiding anything, I think I would know.

She didn't hesitate to say yes. It made me think a little. As far as I was concerned, everyone was guilty, then we would find out soon enough. This is not something the police wanted me to do, but when your only child has been murdered you will do anything to get answers.

I had a taxi pick me up, then we drove into her driveway. When she came out, she was very beautiful. My son was only with her a month; she must know something.

We drove to a nearby restaurant and got a table. It was around 1:00 p.m. and a warm, sunny day. We began talking and she was very calm and collected. I think she was a year older than Brock and seemed very mature.

I didn't get any bad vibes from her at all. For someone who had family problems, she seemed to have it all together. I wasn't going to be fooled, so the lunch continued.

"Did you and Brock have a good relationship?" I asked.

"Yes, we knew each other from high school and reconnected when he came home from Nova Scotia," she replied.

"Did Brock have any enemies that you knew of?" I asked.

"I didn't know of any," she said.

We talked some more and then I had to ask. "Did you love Brock?"

"Yes, I loved him. I was the last one to hold him. We were inside the house and the music was loud when we thought they were taking a long time. When we went outside, they were both lying still on the ground."

THE CELL

John knew from the police that Brock had a friend with him.

"I went over to Brock and held him on the ground. There was a lot of blood. Then I heard him gasp for air. I could hear the others calling for an ambulance." she said calmly.

"Did you try CPR or anything to try and save him?" I asked.

"I just held him, as I could hear the sirens coming. I just held him," she said.

We finished lunch and called for a taxi. There was a lot to think about.

We drove to her house and I got out of the car. I went over to her side and thanked her, then we hugged. She said, "If you need to talk with me, you can call me."

"Thank you," I said.

I had the taxi drop me off and went inside the house. Kim asked me, "How did it go?"

"She's a tough one to figure out. She wasn't nervous at all and didn't stumble on any questions. I found her to be real. I didn't know that she came out on the driveway and saw Brock lying there."

"Yes." Kim said. "She said that she loved him."

"I think she did." Kim replied.

I didn't know who was in shock anymore. Kim and John had met with the police twice already, so they knew more than I did. Brock's girlfriend was very credible to me.

I was going to keep asking questions and run every day into town, past the house where Brock was killed.

You don't sleep at night. You don't know if the house is going to get shot up at night or if there was a bigger plan going on.

Kim and John knew a lot more than me about Brock's behavior since he was at home.

These house parties bothered me. We talked about it after dinner every night.

I started asking a lot more questions. We all had a certain amount of guilt, but we needed to talk. I wanted to know everything. Who was he hanging with? I knew he spent time with his girlfriend, but who else was there? What friends did he have?

Tomorrow was the viewing with open casket, then the funeral on Monday. I would have to watch it online. The funeral home had it on their site.

The funeral home had been very good to us, but there is still a cost. Your son gets murdered and you have to pay money. It doesn't make any sense. None of it does, the way the Province of Ontario was handling things.

Before the viewing and the funeral, there was a time when I got to see my son. I got to see Brock for one hour. Just him and me alone. I burst into tears seeing him and immediately kissed him and tried to hold him. His body was cold and I could feel where they had wrapped his stomach with bandages. For one hour I never took my eyes off of him. I kissed him as many times as I could, his forehead cold as ice.

This is what they had done to my boy! Murdered him in cold blood. Then jumped into their car without asking for any kind of assistance and tried to get as far away from the crime scene as possible. Let him bleed out. Murderers!

The Six Nations was also having a boycott at the same time in Binbrook over townhouse development on their land, so it seemed perfect time to draw attention away from ourselves. We just needed the names or a name.

I continued to run along Binbrook Road and ran into a lady whose son was a friend of Brock's. She was a runner, so we stopped and talked for a few minutes.

"I'm sorry about your son. It was terrible what happened. My son knew your son and they were friends. They all feel guilty about what happened."

I asked her, "What do you mean they all felt guilty?"

"There were others with Brock that day when he got off work. I think you should talk with all of them."

I thanked her and went back to the house. I talked to John and Kim, but they didn't think much about it.

"How can you guys not think much about it?" I asked. "We have no answers from the police, so we have to find them out for ourselves!"

"I don't care who we got to kick the shit out of, but someone is going to pay. That could be more than one!"

It was all getting to be too much for Kim, but John was right there with me. John had to handle Kim; even with the help of Kim's mother, Donna, this was a huge task.

Every time I would have a sit down with Kim and John, I would inevitably get more info from them about Brock's friends or any parties he attended. They seemed to be protecting him, which I understood, but as a father, I was going to turn over every stone to find the truth.

It was nerve-wracking waiting to find out names. I would have two meetings tomorrow — one with the police, alone, and one later on with a group of Brock's friends. The police said they wanted to talk with me alone and maybe get a different perspective.

I waited patiently the next day before the police pulled up. John and Kim had left to do some shopping, and Donna and Jack had stayed in the back. The police sat down at the table, and as I've said before, were very professional with their tone. They know what they're doing, but I was also telling them that I had been talking with people.

I had notes that I had put together and shared them with the police. "Everything you have is right!" said Detective Steve. "We want you to be careful. We have a direction now, and you knocking on doors will not help."

I understood this, but I am his father!

"We can only tell you we have a direction. That is all we can tell you," said Detective David. He seemed like he was now taking the lead position. "We wanted to talk to you without Kim and John. We wanted a different perspective from you. We know you are respected and know a lot of people, but we don't want to see you get in any trouble. Remember: please trust us!"

"Okay, thank you. But what does 'a direction' mean?"

"We can't say a lot right now," David said.

"We are a team," Detective David said. "We'll find them!"

"Okay thank you."

I could see they were using us to feel their way around. They knew that Kim, John and I spoke, and we all had our own theories. All of us thought the killers had to be in the same age range. Why were they there? Maybe they were at another house party, as this seemed to be the norm.

Later, I walked into town and met with a couple of Brock's friends.

One lived above the burger joint where Brock worked. This was also a theory: Maybe it was a customer who was involved. None of the facts pointed to this, but we didn't know yet.

I went upstairs and knocked on the door of Brock's friends. They answered and invited me in. One was very quiet and, from what I knew, had a previous brain injury in an assault case. The other was his girlfriend, who was very cordial and then there was another guy who was all jacked up.

He said, "As soon as we know who they are, we're going to get them."

I told him, "Calm down, because you can miss something right in front of you if you're not paying attention. That's want I you to focus on." The same thing the detectives had told me.

"If we find out a name then we'll take care of it! You guys stay out of trouble!"

I added a little something at the end.

"Don't let me hear that you were involved in any way. I won't be very happy!"

I went back down to the burger joint where Brock had worked and ordered a burger. While I was waiting, a guy came in and picked up an order to go. After he left, the manager told me, "That's the guy who had the house party where Brock was killed."

I told them to hold my order as I slowly left the store. I watched as he went across the street, into his house. I followed him across the street, then, after a minute, I knocked on his door.

When he answered, I said, "My name is Barry Beck. My son, Brock, was killed in your driveway. Can I come in to talk, please?"

Busting my way in wasn't going to get me too far, so I tried the subtle approach.

"Sure. Come on in," he said.

As I followed him in, I saw stacks of empty beer bottles, from ceiling to floor, and could smell the odor of beer in the house. A young kid, maybe 17, came in through the kitchen to join us.

I was pointed to the couch to sit down. There, we began our conversation.

"I've already heard that you want to kill me, or some others want me dead also. I can't do anything about that night."

"So, what happened," I asked.

"I don't know," he said. "We were all inside." I asked the young kid, "How old are you?" He said, "17."

Were you drinking at the party?" I asked.

"Yes, but my mother was here, so I am allowed to drink under provincial law!"

I almost exploded.

"You realize my son was killed — and you're worried about some law, you little punk-ass motherfucker!"

The tone now had changed as I took control of the room. I leaned in and said to the older guy, "Get the young kid back with his family because if I come back and he's still here then you got a big fucking problem! Understand?"

"Yes. I understand," he said.

Then I got up and walked out the door. I thought they knew a lot more than they were telling.

It seemed that's the way it was with everyone. Keep your mouth shut and let the police do their job.

I walked back over and got my burger, then walked home on the side of Binbrook Road. Every day, I learned something new and was slowly filling in the pieces of the puzzle.

After talking with Brock's girlfriend, and then some of his friends, I was starting to put the picture together. The police could only say they had a direction and that they didn't know each other.

What was that 'direction' the police kept saying? John talked with a judge friend of his and this could mean that the police have information, but they needed more to make any arrests. They had to obtain cell phone record data and that was not easy to do in Ontario.

The police were so restricted in Ontario. That's why they told us in the beginning: it could take months. This weighed heavy on me. I felt like I was getting close. I was always a gentlemen when I spoke to people, but if I thought leaning on them could serve me better, well … I did it.

I knew Brock had worked at the burger joint, so I often went there. I just hung out and waited to see the comings and goings of the place. I learned a lot by being there.

I could feel Brock's presence in that joint.

When I walked back to John and Kim's house, I asked them about the passenger Brock had with him that night.

They told me his name is Timmy Walters, and that he had been in trouble with the police before.

||| THE CELL |||

"Why was Brock hanging with him, if he'd been in trouble with the cops," I asked.

"Brock was trying to help him. He had problems," Kim said.

Seemed like everyone had problems here. The circle was getting a little bigger now. I couldn't help but think maybe Brock had gotten mixed up in something that led him down the path to his murder.

The police had said that Brock's passenger was under-age. After the two cars met at the intersection, why wasn't there any video of it? The police maintained that it was a random road rage incident, that the occupants did not know each other.

I found this hard to believe in such a small community. The cops had been doing this kind of research for 25 years, so they must have it right.

I said to John, "Do you know where Timmy Walters lives?"

"Yes" he said.

"Well, let's go, then!"

We jumped in John's car as fast as we could. We drove down Binbrook, past the intersection and the house where Brock was killed, then turned into a complex.

We slowly drove through the complex until we passed the house where Timmy lived.

'Don't stop," I said to John. "Just keep driving slowly."

We drove around the complex twice and then went back to the house.

It was early in the evening. I told John, "I'm going back to Timmy's house. I'm just going to walk."

"You don't want me to come with you?" John asked.

John had been very helpful to me since I arrived. He opened his house to me and treated me like a brother. Kim and John wanted to find the killers as much as I did.

I had a little over a month until I would go back to Vancouver, first to see my friends and mother before going back to Hong Kong. I wanted to have a memorial for Brock there so my friends could pay their respects.

That would mean a lot to me and them — to give a proper goodbye.

I had talked with my brother Murray in the early days of the investigation. He told me not to tell my mother of Brock's murder.

"She won't be able to take it!" he said.

"I have to be the one to tell her," I said.

Both grandmothers were highly involved with Brock's life. So were my brothers and Kim's brothers and stepfather Jack. Kim's grandmother, Jessie, was 99 years old and still had Brock over to her house many times while he was growing up.

It adds up quickly: the devastation inflicted upon our lives. You're never going to be the same. It cuts you deep. A part of you feels dead but the other part keeps pushing. You want the killer or killers bad. It's all you can think about. Revenge first, then we can talk about any forgiveness that follows.

When I did call my mother and tell her of Brock's murder, it was like a piece of us had been ripped away. It took a while before the crying ended and we were able to talk.

The last thing she said to me was, "Barry, don't you be getting into any trouble now. Brock's gone. I can't take both of you gone!"

We were waiting for news every day, and I was walking the back roads to see or feel anything unusual. There were plenty of unusual people in the area that I now knew, but I hadn't filled in the centerpiece of the puzzle yet.

So I set out in the early evening to walk past Timmy Walters' house. It was the same walk I did every day.

I went right to Timmy Walters house. I knocked on the door and could see inside bodies scatter to go upstairs. I knocked a few more times and there was no answer. I decided to leave a note on the car windshield with my Hong Kong number.

John had been letting me use his phone, as a lot of my calls were long distance. If Timmy's mother had seen John's number, then maybe she wouldn't call back.

On the note, I said, "Please call me back."

The police reports had said that Timmy was knocked out right away from an assault, so he didn't know what had happened to Brock. The two cars had met at the intersection, from the police report, around 1:00 am.

There was some kind of exchange, then the other car followed Brock's car back to the party — which was only a couple of blocks away.

They pulled up tight behind Brock's car, then quickly jumped out and attacked Timmy first. The report said that Timmy was unconscious, then Brock had time to grab a golf club from his trunk to strike one of the attackers. From the reports, there were more than three attackers, but the final tally would be five.

After the two weeks of quarantine were up, I was free to move about.

I had been trying to be discreet, but when your son has been stabbed to death, you want quick results. I tried to stay as close to the house as possible, in case any officers came by. No one ever checked on me.

The police told us in the beginning that after 25 years, they still have cold cases. I thought about those families having to wait so long and maybe never finding out what happened to their loved one. It burned me up inside.

What if this happened in Brock's case? I felt I was so close to solving it myself that I could really push hard now.

Kim's mother, Donna, and stepfather, Jack, were going to be leaving the next day for Nova Scotia. That was their home and Brock had been staying a few doors down from their place when attending university. I think they felt better that I was there and would help Kim and John as much as possible.

I felt like a Lone Ranger at times, trying to solve a crime. The possibility of me stumbling upon something was remote.

THE CELL

Everyone seemed to be scared to talk. Maybe the killer was already threatening people before he killed Brock. This was one of our theories: Someone who was intimidating the neighborhood.

The police are smart, and I trusted them. It was a two-way street. They knew I wasn't going to sit still, but they didn't want any more killings going on. Brock had been the 10th person murdered in the Hamilton area that year, which was already a record.

The culture was changing, and I knew that as I watched the news every day from Hong Kong. The USA culture overflows into Southern Ontario and produces this wannabe gangster attitude. That you're an untouchable. This was another theory.

You think of every scenario over and over again, hoping someone breaks. Maybe they drink too much one weekend and start talking to someone. That's why you try to get all the hunters in place. When someone breaks, you hear about it. You hope the police get there first.

If they don't …

Prison Cell

August, 2020

Time was going by fast. Our meetings with police were the same.

They had a direction and would follow it. I prayed they were getting close to someone. When your son has been murdered and you sleep in his room, you become him. You're trying to tell people where the killer is. That's what I was trying to listen for every night.

With Brock's murder, I was thrust into this prison cell of trauma. You can't get out, because you don't have the tools necessary. You're still wanting to kill, so you're trapped like a prisoner, inside the cell, looking at every crack and hole so you can dig your way out.

You can read all the pamphlets you get from social workers. You can look online, but when you're in that cell, it's going to take some time. You're not getting out overnight. This is going to take a lifetime. You can feel it. Can you ever be free?

I would continue on my runs or walks through town. One day, a guy was standing across the street, down a little bit from the house where Brock was murdered. I circled my way around and casually came up behind him.

"How are you today?" I asked.

"Fine, thank you." he replied.

"My name is Barry Beck, and my son, Brock, was killed across the street a couple of weeks ago. Did you happen to hear anything?"

"Well, I don't live here, but I think my buddy and his girlfriend are coming out soon."

This guy and a girl started walking down the stairs toward us. They introduced themselves and we continued the conversation.

"Did you hear anything about my son's murder?" I asked them.

THE CELL

"Well, your son dropped by here around 8:00 pm and brought out a golf club and was threatening me!"

This was all new to me.

"There was four of them in the car. Three guys and a black girl. The other guy in the front seat was Timmy Walters. I know Timmy because he stole my truck before and walks across my property on his way home and tells me to F--- Off!"

This guy Timmy sounded like a bad seed. My son Brock didn't sound much better at the time. The black girl must have been Brock's girlfriend.

Later, I would find out about the other guy in Brock's car. "Did you tell the police of the incident?" I asked.

"Yes," he replied.

I thanked him for being cooperative. They were very friendly towards me, and I thought they were very credible.

I said goodbye and started to walk back to John's house.

What the fuck just happened here? Why the fuck hasn't anyone told me of this incident — not even the police during the interviews we had.

By the time I got back to the house, I was fucking pissed. Both Kim and John were in the front room. I confronted them right away.

"Did you know about the incident down at the house near where Brock was killed?"

"Yes. We knew," John answered.

"Why the fuck didn't anyone tell me?" I fumed.

"There's been so much going on, Barry, I just forgot." John answered.

"How the fuck could you forget this?" I asked.

"I'm sorry, but there's been a lot going on."

"Well, I stopped and talked to the guy and his girlfriend, and they said Brock got out of his car and threatened him with this stupid fucking golf club I keep hearing about. Brock's girlfriend was also with him."

When I went for lunch with her, she didn't mention anything about the incident. This disturbed me.

John and Kim knew of the incident, but they hadn't told me. They obviously knew a lot more about what happened that night than I did.

I knew that Kim was very fragile and in a different state of mind after having her only child murdered. John was also helping her along, so maybe they did forget.

I had to dig into this.

"What's with the golf club?" I asked John.

"Brock had been hitting golf balls in the back yard with a driver when the head of the club went flying off. They all laughed, and Brock threw the club down in a pile of garbage that John was going to take away.

"Brock later came back and put the shaft of the club in his trunk to use as protection." John said.

Okay, Brock was only home for a month, I thought, and he knew he needed protection in the current climate. That part, I could understand because I used to carry around a baseball bat in my own trunk ever since I was 16; but I threw a baseball glove and ball in the trunk — not only to make it look better, but I would play baseball at any time.

Protection, I understood. But he seemed to be the aggressor in this incident.

"What about his girlfriend, Kim? Why didn't she tell me about this? Don't you see how this complicates everything?" I said.

"We knew Brock had been drinking with his friends since he got home from University," she said.

"Well, didn't you talk to him about it?" I asked.

"Yes, we told him not to drink and drive!"

This part was good, but how much was he actually drinking?

Since Brock was home, Kim and John would leave every weekend to go to their personal place they had. That left Brock with the whole house, and John had a lot of toys.

Kim and John came home on a Sunday night and Brock had a few friends over, drinking. Maybe they were smoking pot too. Who knows, as I was a long-distance dad.

Brock had always been truthful with me, but he was now gone. I started to feel this huge responsibility, like I missed everything that Brock was doing. The drinking, the partying — yes, I had done the same thing at his age, but it was a different culture.

The culture now was explosive, so I could see how this could be a big problem. I may have kicked some ass when I was younger, but I was always a gentleman about it. This wasn't Brock's personality. Hanging with Timmy Walters wasn't going to help, so why was he doing it?

Was he trying to help him? Or did he just want friends? Any kind of friends? He was a smart kid, but in a short period of time was doing things that could get him in trouble.

I told Kim and John, "Don't you see this is our responsibility first? It starts here with us! Yes, I understand Brock was murdered, but we could have done more! We're a fucking team, and will be all the way through this for the rest of our lives."

Brock wasn't a kid anymore. Every day, I would hear some kind of news that either the police couldn't tell me because it was an ongoing investigation or Kim and John had so much going on, being there and living it every day, that they just forgot. I could see how harrowing it was for them.

John was trying to help Kim, and she needed it. We all did, but Kim wouldn't accept that Brock was gone. It was hard to manage, and I understood them.

I wanted to talk with Brock's girlfriend again, so I sent her a message about the incident. She told me that she kept yelling at Brock to get back in the car, which he did.

THE CELL

She then went on and said it had something to do with Timmy but she didn't know. It had been Brock's last night of work, and he got off at 7:00 pm. The incident happened around 7:30 and Brock was murdered in the early morning at 1:30 the next day. That was only six hours later.

The puzzle was being filled in a little more. I would question everyone and called to talk with the police again. The police don't just drop everything and come running. They're working the case and understand the needs of the families engulfed in trauma. There was a social worker who became very helpful. She helped the families affected by trauma. She would be the one who I corresponded with the most.

John went directly to the police. We couldn't both be working the same angles as we talked about this in the very beginning.

When the police did come, they were very composed. They could tell us a little more about trying to get cell phone records and how hard the government protects the accused more than the victims. The problem was, there hadn't been anyone accused yet.

I did trust the police. I also trusted Kim and John. I told both of them that I wanted to know everything. I had been in Hong Kong for 14 years.

That weighed heavily on me. John and Kim knew that, so we all had to take equal responsibility if we had missed something.

You look at everyone again and again. Did I miss something? You need to stand back and breathe, but there was no time to do that.

John's phone rang and he said, "It's for you Barry."

It was Timmy's mother. She had finally answered the note I had left on her car. I was very respectful towards her.

I asked her if we could get together and talk. I could hear her kids in the background. "It's Barry Beck. It's Barry Beck."

She agreed to meet at a restaurant. I told Kim and John that I wanted to go alone. We set a time for the next day. The time was 6:00 pm. She had to work so this would give her more time. She sounded like she wanted to help.

I was excited for the meeting. Timmy seemed to be the key to Brock's murder.

The problem was, he was a minor. Kim and John didn't know this at first. Brock was 20 years old. Why was he hanging in this group with Timmy? It got more complicated each day.

The police had questioned him in the hospital the next day after Brock's murder. He had sustained a concussion and other head injuries.

I wasn't sympathetic.

I went to the restaurant at 5:45 pm to meet Timmy's mother. John gave me his phone in case she would call.

I waited until 7:30 pm. She did not show up.

I tried to call her several times, with no answer.

I went back to the house dismayed. John and Kim were waiting for me.

"What happened," John asked.

"She didn't show," I replied.

"I knew it!" John said.

The next day, she called and said she was sorry and got tied up at work. I asked for another meeting, to which she agreed. I told her she could come over to the house and I would have Kim and John leave. I thought she would be more comfortable.

She accepted and we set the time for the next evening.

John and Kim left, so it was just me at the house. I waited an hour past the time and finally a car pulled into the driveway. It was summer, so I had left the door open. I thought it would be more inviting.

I looked out the door and it was Kim and John.

She called the next day with another excuse. I said it was okay and never raised my voice with her. I told her that it was important that we meet; your son was with Brock when he was killed.

Please meet me, I asked. She agreed again. John had told me that she wouldn't come. "She's scared!" he said.

I understood. I guess I would be, too, but I would think that it would be part of my responsibility. We set the time the next day and once again she did not show or call. I tried calling several times, but there was no answer.

When John came back, I said "Let's go now, please, over to Timmy's house!"

We jumped into the car and headed over there. Her truck was gone and there was a padlock on the front door. We drove around several times but didn't see her truck or any movement in the house. She was gone and so were the kids. You're running on adrenaline but getting no answers.

Filling in the center of the puzzle was now at a standstill.

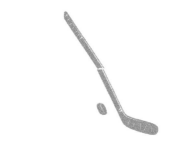

The Tornado

Kim and John told me I could stay as long as I wanted, but we all knew the arrests could take some time. I felt like I had done everything I could. The police handling the case, Steve Bereziuk and David Brewster, had no new info, and it could take some time.

Although I had differed with some of the decisions made by Kim and John, we were all still grieving. I had come to respect John for the love he displayed for Kim and the way he welcomed me under the circumstances. It was a horrible time, but through it all there was love between the three of us. I felt like we were so close to finding someone. We had everyone looking. Fuck, we wanted them bad!

After Brock was murdered, the decision was made to have his body cremated. We had gone by the funeral home and picked out an urn that we felt reflected Brock's personality. There also was a display of smaller urns for other family members.

We decided on an urn, and a smaller one for me that I could take and have a piece of Brock with me. On the way home, in the car, I put the bigger urn between my legs so it wouldn't tip over. I held it close and tight. That's the process of cremation. The funeral home takes care of it, but when you hold your son's urn, it rattles you to your core!

When you have to pay the funeral home for everything they've done, there's a bill that you've got to take care of. Even when they give you extra help and try to alleviate some of the cost and pain, you still have to pay. This part fucking made me angry. The funeral home were good people, but it's the fucking bill you get when your son's been murdered that hits you hard.

You are continuously paying as you go along. It didn't make any sense to me. PAY, PAY, PAY and you keep paying. You want to punch the wall as hard as you can … or kill somebody!

Brock was my investment. That's what I used to tell him. "I don't invest in stocks or gold, because you are my investment!" He would laugh, and that's what stuck with me: his laugh.

||| **THE CELL** |||

When you get a chance to stop and think, you're a punching bag. You keep getting hit from all sides. My son was just getting started and now it was all over. "Why Me?" you keep asking. "Why has my God forsaken me?"

I was trying to be the strong one. It's what I knew, but in your private moments, you melt into the hands of God. Jesus Christ was my savior because I'd been saved before, but when I lay in Brock's bed, I questioned if there even was a God.

"If I'd been saved, was this the cost I had to pay?" The depth of pain that you have to endure every day, every moment. All the unanswered questions. You're inside the prison cell and it's powerful. Like a tornado. You pray that it will lead you somewhere. It's a higher power that you're now experiencing first-hand. You have to know. "Why Me?" You are naked and have nothing but have everything.

Filling in the puzzle would have to wait, and so would all the unanswered questions.

I was spinning inside the tornado and hoped it would spit me out somewhere good.

Just release me from this prison cell.

I felt that "Why Me?" would change. It couldn't stay like that. I would need to interpret it a different way:

"Why not me?"

The meaning for me became to serve. That's how I could keep my son's legacy continuing, not be killing anyone — although that will be the last part to leave my head … possibly.

Vancouver Memorial

September, 2020

It was time to leave Binbrook. The unanswered questions I would leave in the hands of the police and Kim and John. TRUST was a big word.

Saying goodbye to Kim and John would be difficult. There were so many emotions that I had to deal with. I didn't want to feel hate anymore.

There would be one more sleep in Brock's bed. When I crawled into bed that night I wrapped the sheets around me tightly. I only wanted to feel love. It was another sleepless night that I didn't want to end.

John knocked on my door early in the morning. I was already awake and packing. I took the small urn and placed it in my handbag. I'd been given a document from the funeral home so I could carry it with me back to Hong Kong. I was first going to Vancouver to see my friends, then to Osoyoos to see my mother.

It was an empty feeling when the car arrived. John and Kim didn't want me to leave. We all hugged and cried one more time together. It was like being torn apart.

John put my bags in the trunk and we hugged one more time. It was our first time meeting, and we both deeply felt the effect of Brock's death. I loved John, as he was willing to do anything to help the situation. He made me feel as comfortable as possible.

I got into the car and held my handbag with Brock's urn close to me. I looked back at Kim and John until I couldn't see them anymore. Just felt empty now.

As we pulled onto the highway, I made conversation with the driver and also went through all the notes I'd come up with. Like I said, I had the outside of the puzzle filled in; but for the inside, I needed more people talking — and that didn't happen. I think most people were of the adage that the police will do their work.

I think they were right: We would have to rely on the police or on our hunters.

THE CELL

As we neared the Toronto airport, I actually felt a surge of strength. I would be going to Vancouver to have a memorial for Brock that my friends Trish and Ange would set up above their condominium complex. I would also be staying at their posh condo and be among friends. That was most important to me: to be with friends. I could draw strength from them.

The flight from Toronto to Vancouver is five hours but it seemed like a short one because of the excitement I felt. You looked to draw strength from anywhere, but friends are the ones who do it. In my case, this is the way it was.

At the airport, I was picked up by Ange and Big R. It was good to see them. We hugged each other. They both gave me their condolences as we rushed out to the parking lot.

As we got in the car, Ange said, "Barry, we're so sorry. But when you're here you stay with Trish and I!"

Then Big R said, "I'll do anything for you, Bubba!"

It was overwhelming — the emotions and how they were changing. I was looking forward to the memorial and seeing friends. Feeling the warmth and love was going to help me, although it would still be an emotional night.

As we headed to Ange's condo in Burnaby, we made a few stops to pick up items for dinner. Mostly steaks for the party. That's what it was becoming — a party for Brock.

I liked where this was headed. Sure, there would be sadness, but we would have laughter and warmth as much as possible. This, for me, was part of my healing: Being in the comfort of family and friends.

I think Trish and Ange lived on the 47th floor of their building. They had a beautiful condo, with expansive views of the city and North Shore mountains. We had barely got inside when Trish was anxious to show me upstairs, but we kept hugging each other. There was so much love after all the hate in Binbrook and I welcomed it.

I had a few hours before the memorial, so Trish made something for us to eat. She loved to cook and both Ange and I loved to eat.

After we ate, there was time for a short rest and I lay down to admire the view. Brock and I had spent a lot of time in Vancouver. It would be a special night.

I thought of the night ahead, and also of my youth growing up in Vancouver. I wasn't asking myself, 'Why Me?" There was something more that lay ahead. Something that I felt I would have to do. Yes, I would be waiting for the police or John to call me every day, but I wanted some peace and love. That's what was going to help my healing process.

Trish and Ange asked me if I wanted to go up to the site. I excitedly agreed. "Wow" as I walked through the doors. There was a 360-degree view on a beautiful Vancouver day. Mt. Baker, to the east, looked so clear and close.

Vancouver Memorial

We walked around the whole space and marveled at it. Trish had also told me that she invited people to come at sunset. We went back and forth to Ange's place to move some items up for the party. It was a memorial to Brock but became more of a celebration party of Brock's life.

As the guests arrived, it was a very casual atmosphere. I wished John and Kim could experience this and get them out of Binbrook for a while. They were in it and living it every day. It tears at you and breaks you down. You need to acquire strength and courage to fight it.

I had many friends who attended the memorial/party for Brock.

Childhood friends, and friends I came to know along the way. The McKinney family of Denise, Brian and my great friend Donny Silas McKinney. We grew up on the same block and were like family. The Ferraros, with Ronny 'Big R' Ferraro and his wife Maria and kids Sabrina (My God-daughter) and Emilio. Elementary school friends Mitch Ponak and his wife, Marcie, along with good friend, Ron Petriska. My brother Murray. Musician friend Mike Kalanj. Former New Westminster Bruin teammate Mark Lofthouse, his wife, and Dan Clark, who played for Kamloops. My good friend Dino Rosa and so many others.

I was informally introduced by Angelo, and then thanked everyone. It was emotional to see all the faces there to support me. I told a short story of Brock and then just wanted everyone to enjoy themselves. Ange and Trish had done a lot of work preparing this gathering, and it was such a beautiful night. I felt all the love, and that gave me strength. Everyone helped me to be strong. I wanted this night to last forever, but we had a planned trip to see my mother in Osoyoos early in the morning. It was a beautiful night riding on a high of emotion.

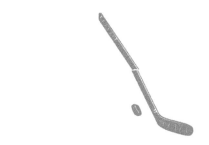

Osoyoos Bound

September, 2020

In the morning, we started to get ready for the trip to Osoyoos to see my mother and friends. Ange had to call the car rental agency and ask for a Suburban, as there would be five of us going: Ange, Silas, Mitch, Big R and myself. Taking Highway 1, then Highway 3, is one of the most scenic drives in British Columbia.

We were only going for two nights, but were excited for the trip as we piled into the Suburban. It was a road trip that we all needed. The topography changes quickly on Highway 3. You head out into the mountains, past the famous Hope Slide and into the protected Manning Park.

"Wow," I thought, "it really is like it says on the license plate: 'Beautiful British Columbia!'"

Everything seemed to be a healer for me. From my friends to nature — and we knew the best was yet to come. We became close on the drive, and I could feel the love.

When we arrived at Osoyoos, I could feel the dry desert heat. It's often over 40 C (104 degrees Fahrenheit) during the summer, and is well-known for its orchards and wine. It also boasts the warmest lake in all of Canada, Lake Osoyoos, and is located 2 km (1.24 miles) from the U.S. border.

The first stop was to see my mother, as the seniors residence, Mariposa Gardens, was just at the start of the highway as we drove through. There were COVID restrictions in place, so my mother could only see one person. There was an outside area where she waiting, sitting down.

Ange pulled the truck up and I got out. My mother stood up and waved to everyone, as she knew them all well. I was only allowed to stay for an hour, so the guys went to the hotel to arrange the rooms.

One of the rules was there was no touching, but when I got close to my mother, I hugged her tight. I could feel her resistance at first, and then we held each other firmly and cried. We cried because we so thrilled to see each other, and we cried for our loss of Brock.

We stopped crying long enough for my mother to say, "He was like a son to me, too, you know!"

"Yes, Mom. I know."

I helped her sit down, then we began to talk.

"Have the police found out anything yet?" she asked.

"Nothing yet, Mom, but they will."

We consoled each other through the conversation as the hour flew by before one of the staff came out and told us our time was up. I called Ange to come and pick me up. As the staff went inside, I hugged my mother once more and told her I would be back in the morning.

She was close to Brock; he called her often. You can never use the word "Devastating" enough, but I could feel it inside her.

Ange arrived and he came over briefly to say hello to my mother. She didn't want us to leave, but an hour was all that was allowed. I hugged her again, then Ange and I got back in the vehicle. She stayed and watched us as we drove away. We both waved as Ange pulled out of the parking lot. It was another step in a positive direction as we headed to the hotel.

It was only a short drive through town, so there wasn't time to think a lot. Just enjoy everything now.

It was still before noon, and Mitch wanted to see if we could rent a boat. We got everything together quickly, and I grabbed some fruit and mini-cereal boxes from the breakfast area. We piled into the Suburban and headed down Lakeshore Drive. There would be plenty of places to rent a boat.

We stopped at Walnut Grove Resort and checked out the boats for rent. Mitch took charge, as he was a fishing boat captain and knew the ropes.

He found a new pontoon boat and said, "What about this one?" "Oh, yes, Mitchy!" Ange said. "There's enough room for all of us!"

I don't know if Mitch had this planned or not, but it was a great idea. It was hot and sunny, and being on the lake was the perfect place. We could rent the boat for an hour, as it was reserved after us.

I came prepared.

We jumped onto the boat. Big R, Silas, Ange, myself and Mitch in the driver's seat. As Mitch drove us away from the rental area, the hot sun beat down on us. We took off our shirts, as it was the perfect day. Mitch gave the engines a little juice and we could feel the warm breeze. It was not far until we came to where my parents' house was — the house we had all been to, the house where my parents had retired to from Vancouver, the house where Brock had spent a large part of his youth, playing and being a kid.

Mitch slowly stopped the boat. There was a tray on a shelf and I began to pull items out of my bag. The fruit, mini-cereal boxes that Brock used to eat for breakfast, and Brock's urn that I had in my bag.

It was quiet now and our only thoughts were on Brock. After placing the items on the tray, I started to walk to the front of the boat. Everyone was looking when I said, "I think this is the perfect spot to release some of Brock's urn, and I have some fruit and other things that you can place in the water for him."

To me, this would give him a safe journey into God's arms and comfort him. One by one, each of us would take an item and place it in the calm water and say a short prayer.

First, the other guys placed the fruit, then the cereal, and I had some flowers that they also placed before a short prayer. We were all crying when it came to my turn.

I took some fruit, cereal, flowers that were on the tray.

I took out some money and placed that on top of the water.

I knelt as close as could be to the water, my face about six inches away.

I said a short prayer.

"My Father, please bless my son on this journey he now takes and comfort him."

I got up for a second to take some money out of my pocket. I placed that in the water, to signify wealth on Brock's journey.

I knelt and talked closely over the water.

I slipped off my B.C. Hall of Fame ring that I was so proud of, leaned over the boat and dropped it into the water.

I watched as it sank slowly down to the bottom. The water was murky, so it didn't take long to disappear.

I then took Brock's urn and emptied some of the contents into the water, watching as it floated away.

I once again began crying. I dove into the water.

I went down as deep as I could before coming back up again.

Upon grabbing a breath, I noticed I was in the middle of the flowers.

I guess I dove into the water to be closer to Brock. It made sense to me at the time. To be with my son in the water was as close as I was going to get to him now.

I swam in the water slowly, trying to feel him. Then I went to the back of the boat, where there was a ladder Mitch pulled down so I could climb out.

It was an experience unlike any I'd had before. A sense of rebirth came over me.

We all cried and hugged one another, then Mitch turned the motor back on and we headed back. We'd completed the memorial that was so special for my family, myself and my friends included.

After getting off the boat, we were all on a bit of a high, so we decided to go visit a couple of friends.

||| THE CELL |||

First, it was Jimmy Liebel, as he was up near Fernando's fruit market and Ange was trying to bring back 500 pounds of tomatoes for his parents to make tomato sauce. He stopped in quickly and made a deal to come back early in the morning.

Then we drove to see Jimmy and Cyndi Liebel. They had a beautiful place with grass that felt like it was golf-course quality. He had a water display feature and sat up on a hill.

After showing us around, we all went up and sat on the deck for a while and just talked. We talked about Brock, as Jimmy had coached him in minor hockey. We were able to laugh once again and enjoy the good times of Brock living in Osoyoos.

After visiting Jimmy, it wasn't too far before we came to Wayne Pendergraf's place. Wayne had also coached Brock, and we often spent time with each other as we coached the peewee team together. We were also friends and did a lot of fishing up on a pond he had on the property.

We were enjoying the moment and would reflect back to Brock. At certain times, Wayne used to take me, Brock, and his girls Miranda and Taylor, down to the Omak Rodeo over the border to get a little of Omak culture — which was very Hispanic as well as a lot of native people.

The day was starting to get long, so we asked Wayne to join us at dinner. We had asked Jimmy, too, but he had family plans already.

We went back to the Best Western, had a shower and got ready for dinner.

The Diamond was one of my favorite restaurants in Osoyoos, owned by Gus and Maria. They had always supported minor hockey, along with their son, Micheal, who played and now worked in the restaurant.

Wayne would come and meet us for dinner, as well as his estranged wife, Wanda, who I was friendly with also. They had been a big part of Brock's life while he lived and went to school in Osoyoos.

Ken and Karen Sieben, our next-door neighbors, were also great friends, but when we had stopped to see them, Karen only let me in the front door. Ken was sick from liver damage and had lost a lot of weight. He struggled to talk but at least made several attempts before I decided to leave.

It was "Aunty Karen and Uncle Ken" to Brock. They loved him like a son. They all did — that's why I needed to come to Osoyoos: to give them some closure along with my mother.

I think it was *The Diamond* the first night, then *Campo Marina* the second night. We partied like we were teenagers, but never forgot what our mission was: To spread the love of Brock and give this great town of Osoyoos with all our family friends some closure. The killers weren't caught yet but it didn't dampen the celebration of Brock's life.

On the third night, it was time to leave. We went over to see Al at *The Sage Pub* to say hello, but most of us were burned out from all the partying and hot sun.

Osoyoos Bound

We said hello to Al and were only in there for an hour. We all wanted to go back to the hotel and sleep, because Mitch had another day planned tomorrow when we got back to Vancouver.

All Ange could think about was loading up that 500 pounds of tomatoes from the Fernandez fruit market. Most of the orchards had changed over to wine, because there was more money in it. For Canada, Osoyoos is where the Okanagan Valley starts. The Sonoran Desert begins in Nevada and sweeps its way up through Eastern Washington right through Osoyoos. Lots of sand dunes and rattlesnakes in Osoyoos.

We had a big breakfast together before stopping to see my mother. The guys waited in the Suburban, and my mom waved hello. This part was hard again. I walked back with my mom to the safe place they had set up. We hugged and cried some before I whispered in her ear, "It's gonna be all right, Mom. Brock is in a safe place now!"

She cried some more along with me as the guys in the Suburban only watched.

I kissed her and told her, "I'll be back as soon as I can, Mom. I promise."

I walked back to the truck and jumped in. I could see my mom crying, still sitting there, so I jumped out and ran over towards her.

As I held her in my arms she said to me, "Be careful Barry! I can't lose you, too!"

"Don't worry, Mom. There will be justice," I said.

"Please don't hurt anyone," she said as I left.

I got back in the truck. Everyone said goodbye as Mitch, who was now driving, pulled out onto Highway 3.

I felt it was a duty fulfilled, and getting to see my mother and friends was a bonus if I could have one. This was turning into a trip of a lifetime, and I needed to feel the love. That's what it was all about: LOVE!

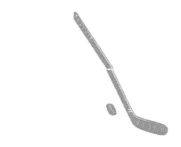

Copper Cove

September, 2020

The drive down to Vancouver on Highway 3 was just as beautiful as the drive up. We all had a sense of accomplishing a mission and everyone did their part. We now felt anxious to get home.

The four-hour drive went quickly, as it always does. You're mesmerized by the beauty of the country and realize you're bound to it. You may live in the city, but this is who you really are.

We first went and dropped off the tomatoes to Ange's parents. Wow!

They were thrilled to see all those tomatoes.

Then we dropped off Silas first, then Big R. Mitch then dropped off Ange, and I and took the truck and drove off.

I asked Ange, "What's going on?"

He said, "At 2:00 p.m., we're going out on Mitch's 90-foot Seiner fishing boat to have another party!"

His boat was docked down at False Creek Marina, a part of Vancouver that they had reconstructed and made into a beautiful marina.

Ange, Trish and I jumped into Ang's truck and drove down as fast as we could. People were already on Mitch's boat, setting up the party.

There would be fresh prawns, steak and salmon. Tuna with salmon sushi and plenty of booze.

The weather was perfect. It was hard to think. Everything was moving so fast. Close friends would be going out on the ocean to have fun and pay respects to my son. I felt the love and the healing.

This would be the third memorial for Brock. Oh, how I missed him, but the love I was surrounded by was overwhelming. This would be the final touch.

THE CELL

Everyone was on as Mitch, the skipper, pulled the vessel out of False Creek Marina. Slowly we went through the marina, gliding by Sunset Beach to the opening to English Bay. We felt the wind and I could feel Brock. He seemed to be all around as Mitch hit the throttle.

I thought about Pav, and how we used to talk about the psychiatric facility that he was in as the "Cuckoo's Nest!" Mitch's boat would provide an excellent setting for it.

Pav was always in my thoughts, even while I focused on Brock. I always thought of them together.

Mitch had hit the tide right as we rounded Lighthouse Park, famously known for its rough water. We went by Whytecliff Park, then Mitch started to slow the boat down.

Just imagine the most beautiful day you've ever experienced, and this is what the past four days had been like for me.

Slowly, we came to a stop outside the house where I used to live.

Silas had lived with me more out of companionship than anything. We had grown up on the same block, and a more dedicated friend you would never find. I had a deep history with everyone on the boat.

Mitch stopped in what was known as Copper Cove.

He lowered the back end, and Ange helped me to prepare the same way we had in Osoyoos. Ange, Mitch, Silas and Big R. Oh, what a crew to have!.

I edged myself to the bottom of the boat, hung onto the side and began to speak.

"I can't thank everyone enough for the love you have shown me, my son Brock and my family. It's such a beautiful day, and I'm so happy we could share it together."

Each person came down beside me one by one. Ange came down to make sure nobody fell in.

Trish and Marci, Mitch's wife, had brought a lot of flowers as an offering to Brock for a safe journey.

It was a peaceful moment, with music playing in the background on the calm cove.

Flowers were placed into the cove as a few seagulls buzzed the boat.

If you wanted to say a prayer, you did. There were a lot of tears shed.

It finally was my turn.

I carefully pulled Brock's urn from my bag.

I knelt close to the water, with Ange holding my arm.

I placed the rest of the flowers into the water, then reached in my pocket and put some money next to the flowers.

I gently unscrewed the top of the urn.

I reached down to the water and poured some of Brock's ashes in. Then I said the prayer that i learned from my mother and she taught Brock before his bedtime.

Now I lay me down to sleep,
I pray the Lord my soul to keep, If I should die before I wake,

I pray the Lord my soul to take.
Rest well, my son, and justice will come.

Mitch started the boat and slowly turned back towards False Creek. The sun was setting as we all hugged each other.

Love, so much love.

When we got back to False Creek, there was a sense of accomplishment. Three memorials. Three parties, for Brock and for us. Surrounded by love.

When Mitch pulled into False Creek, everyone said their goodbyes. I had one more night, as I would leave the next day for Hong Kong.

We went back to Ange and Trish's place and decided to eat at the Cactus Club in the Brentwood area. It was time to wind down, as now the focus would soon shift to when the arrests would be made in my son's murder case.

Before we went out, my phone rang. It was Pav. "Everything going all right, Bubba?"

He was the one now checking up on me.

"We had some great services, and I got to feel so much love from my friends, Pav. You would have loved it!"

To go from hate and then to love so quickly, that's the emotions you have to constantly deal with. For now, it was love and compassion.

I take my hat off to my friends from East Vancouver, where I grew up, who came to support and love me with what I'm going through.

At the first memorial, Silas's sister, Denise, who has been like a sister to me my whole life, said a prayer on behalf of Brock and myself. She mentioned Kim and John and how heartbroken we all were. She didn't dwell there. She built us back up and knew there was going to be a legacy with Brock and how he would never be forgotten.

She told the truth. People don't want to hear the truth about death, but it's merely the circle of life. When it comes to the murder of my own son, the circle stops at me!

Hong Kong S.A.R.
September, 2020

In the morning, we got up and Trish had made us coffee. Ange and I would go pick up Big R, then head to the airport. My Canadian trip was over; it ended as positively as could be, There would be some rough times to battle yet, but being in Vancouver gave me the strength and courage to go on.

Talking with Stan Smyl and Ernie (Punch) McLean gave me an added boost, along with teammate Mark Lofthouse. We'd been through a lot together in our years in New Westminster.

The love and compassion is what kept me going. For this, I will be forever grateful to my friends from East Vancouver.

I knew I would need counseling somewhere along the line, but everything was moving too fast. Just get from Point A to Point B and deal with it as it comes.

The flight to Hong Kong was 13 hours, flying west against the trade winds, so it gave me time to analyze all that had taken place. The unanswered questions about Brock's murder:

His behavior, while only being home for a month from an excellent two years at university in Nova Scotia.

The friends he was associating with.

The night he was murdered.

How did the road rage incident happen?

Once back in Hong Kong, I went straight back to work. I always felt acceptance from the kids I taught, so the rink was my home. It always had been, wherever it was.

At practice, the kids would come up and some would say they're sorry about what happened to Brock. Others would just say Hi. That was enough for me.

||| THE CELL |||

Some parents would say hello, so it was welcoming, but I always felt an edge to being there. I'd have to get comfortable quickly, but that edge never went away. I didn't understand it.

I would never be the same after having my son murdered, but would have to make some kind of understanding of it to ever laugh again and have relationships — which I longed for.

It was four months before my phone rang. I saw Joh's number on it.

"They got them. The bastards. They finally got them!"

"Slow down, John. What's going on," I replied.

"The police have arrested four young men and charged them with Murder 2."

So many times my heart had sunk, but now I was elated.

"Four of them?"

"Yes. The Hamilton Major Crime Unit had the correct info to make the arrests. This is fucking awesome, Barry! We did it!!"

I said, "Okay, let's see where this leads us!"

Inside, I was torn. So many events went wrong that night.

The next call I received was from the prosecutor introducing himself and saying, "We will do everything we can to get a conviction. There has been four arrests, but I must tell you there will be some challenges in this case. We'll talk about them later."

I knew most of the challenges already: No real video of the crime. No witnesses. No murder weapon.

I thought that with all this information, and the prosecutor explaining the reality of the case, we would be lucky to get one of these guys.

I received most of the news from on-line networks. When the police called, they were calm, as usual.

"We got them, Barry. Now comes prosecuting them!"

They had done a great job, but for now their involvement would be reduced. This was the problem of the Ontario Provincial Government and their liberal laws that reduced the abilities of the police to make arrests.

Going forward, we felt the victims had limited rights while the accused had all the rights provided to them from the government. I was furious at all this!!

My phone calls to mayor Fred Eisenberger went to a very helpful and informative assistant, but the mayor did not actually phone or come and see us. The same was true with an informative assistant: no return call.

What the heck were they doing? When a young man gets murdered in your district, you had better go see them and offer your condolences! This never happened and made me upset to no end. They should be supporting the families. "Screw them!" I said.

As the days went by, the names of the accused finally came out.

Thomas Vasquez

||| Hong Kong S.A.R. |||

Albin Gashi
Cam-Thai Khath
Petar Kunic
This is what we had been waiting for.
I immediately called my close loving friend in New York, Marie Etts.
She always found a way to gather info.

Marie had found photos of everyone except Vasquez. She found them all on FaceBook, and photos of their families.

Google Maps showed where they lived, and also the addresses of their businesses

They all were living an extravagant lifestyle. Everyone but Vasquez!

The Wanna-Be Gangsta!
July, 2021

I had great compassion overall for people, but when your son is murdered, there's another side to you that you have to come to terms with.

Religion can be very powerful and dangerous. I always believed in a higher power, but what was it? Was it truly God and his son Jesus Christ, my savior? Yes, I did believe in my faith, and it was sometimes the only thing I had to hold on to.

Not having any info on Vasquez disturbed me. That meant something to me.

"Why would he make it hard for people to find him?"

With the others, it was quite easy. They were all being held without bail until the defense lawyers started to get to work.

I was in Hong Kong, so any communication would be by Zoom. There were many supporters, but one day it all came crashing down — one of those days when you just want to crawl into bed and pull the covers up.

When the phone rang, I didn't want to answer, but I said 'hello' anyway.

It was George McPhee, now president with the Vegas Golden Knights

"How you doing, Bubba?" he asked.

I broke down a little and told him, "Am trying, George, but it's difficult."

"You'll get through it. I know you will!"

We all played together with the Rangers. Pav, George, Gresch, Rexi, Nicky, Laidlaw, Duguay and Dore. I had just gotten through with another overseas call, with good friend Marie Etts, so there are times when emotionally you are on that ride and don't know how to stop it.

George was concerned and professional about the call. It was great to hear from him.

THE CELL

Pav was now the one who was in constant contact with me. He was a brother looking after his brother. I didn't worry about calling Pav, as now my phone was ringing from him. He sounded good.

With help from Clint Malarchuk, Jean Pavelich, Tom Gorence and Jerry Jormakka, as well as his legal team, Pav was now being released into the capable hands of Melony Butler at *The Eagles Landing Nest* — otherwise known as *The Nest* to the veterans who made up the percentage of personnel.

It was overwhelming to know that Pav was free from the psychiatric facility and into a more-open place of love and respect. He would follow their curriculum but now could have his dog, Taz, with him. He was finally in a good place.

I was in almost-daily contact with Kim and John, also.

There wasn't a lot of info coming from the press, and we were frustrated on this part.

We were told if bail hearings came up that there would be more released in the hearings.

At the hockey rink, I could at least clear my mind for what little time there was. Other than that, it was confiding in my friends. There was help from them. You had to talk about it and not hold it all inside. I punched many pillows but tried to remain calm in public. You still tried to laugh but it was intermittent. It was a struggle. I needed help but was too caught up in everything to see it.

I always looked forward to Pav's calls. Now I was the one who needed his support. He called as often as possible, but I soon realized we were all entwined together: Kim, John, Mark, Jean and myself. We all needed professional help, but Mark was the only one getting it.

The rest of us were working on behalf of Brock and Mark, but weren't making time for ourselves. Just waiting for news and going to work wasn't good enough. We were all hurting. Marie was a solid rock for Kim, John and me. Especially for me.

Waiting for the bail hearings was consuming our strength.

Cam Khath would have the first bail hearing. It was done by Zoom, and my camera angle was only to see the judge. I couldn't see the people that were allowed in the courtroom due to COVID restrictions.

I would listen intently as the lawyers and the Crown viewed their positions.

There was new info at the hearing.

Mr. Khath first came to speak, putting up $200,000 in bail money for his son, Cam.

Mr. Khath was of Cambodian descent, and it was difficult to hear him at times. There were bail requirements to be met and he agreed to them all. He and his family had escaped the Khmer Rouge movement and emigrated to Canada.

Once he gave his statements, his sister was then called up. She was crying while she answered questions. managed to see both of them from my angle. I felt sadness and anger at the same time. Sad for the genocide caused by the Khmer Rouge movement that their family may have been involved in. Anger from their son/nephew being involved in my son's murder.

Cam Khath's bail was allowed, and he would be released.

When Kim and John came home they were both in tears. Their home was only 30 minutes from the courthouse. John said, "It was just too easy!"

I did hear early in the hearing that everyone involved was drunk. It was confirmed later in the hearing by the judge.

John mentioned that Cam Khath was a big guy. Very athletic looking. I knew that from his photos. We knew where he had to stay while out on bail. Ideas ran through our heads, but we also discussed what kind of legacy would be left for Brock. We wanted something good to happen from such a tragic event.

After listening through the bail hearing, I felt the judge would release Cam Khath. I didn't hear enough evidence. Yes, he was there, but the Crown couldn't prove much more than that.

I had a bad feeling coming over me. What was the 'direction' the police kept telling us about?

Jaskiran Grewal: Inside Help

July, 2021

When I heard of the second bail hearing with Gashi and Kunic, I was apprehensive. But I knew it was coming. The judge in the first hearing didn't seem to care for what the Crown had to say, although Kunic was also looking at an assault charge on Timmy Walters.

If I went onto the courtroom Zoom early for the hearings, you could learn a lot. It wasn't blacked out, and you could hear the crown counsel preparing.

I never felt positive at any point. I trusted the police, and they did their job well. Then you hear of the procedures in the early stages.

The police have to hand over the evidence to the Crown and then to the defense lawyers. They digest it, then the Crown and the defense meet with the judge and discuss the evidence. COVID seemed to always delay the proceedings.

During this time, we received great support from Jaskiran Grewal, a victim/witness services worker. She helped us tremendously in trying to remain positive under the circumstances. I had many conversations with her, and she was professional all the way. She was our voice to the Crown, Gordon Akilie.

The police, David Brewster and Steve Bereziuk, the Crown and Jaskiran were involved in many family cases, and they were understanding to our emotions. They had dealt with these cases for years.

Talking and communication was essential for us, because we wanted answers. Jaskiran was always there for us. Solid as could be. The police always restricted, as the investigation was ongoing.

THE CELL

At the Zoom hearing for Gashi and Kunic, I listened carefully. Kim and a friend were in the courtroom. There is new info constantly, so you have to listen closely because at times the sound may not be good.

Kim is hearing-impaired and was livid at the hearings. She is hard to control when she's angry. She wanted to be in the courtroom, but she always had to have someone there with her. She voiced her disapproval for a hand translator.

I once again was asked by the judge, "Mr. Beck, can you see and hear on the Zoom account?"

"Good morning, Your Honor. Yes, I can see and hear you."

It was 11:00 pm for me but 11:00 am at the Hamilton Courthouse — twelve or thirteen hours difference with Daylight Savings Time.

The defense and Crown this time became somewhat heated in their exchanges. The defense pointed out again that everyone was drunk at the time of Brock Beck's death, and this became an issue.

It was what I heard next that numbed me from head to toe.

The defense said, "Your Honor, Mr. Gashi has already stated that he heard Thomas Vasquez say, 'I got him, I got him real good!'"

These were the words of a killer. Thomas Vasquez. Brock was tall, but very slender. The stabbing motions of Thomas Vasquez would have torn right through him. Which they did.

Vasquez meant to kill my son.

I threw my earpieces to the floor and got up from my chair. "That Motherf," I said. "I'll kill him myself!"

I put my earpieces back in and got back onto Zoom. I was enraged and knew if Kim heard that she would have burst out in the courtroom.

The hearing continued, so at the time, she didn't hear what was said.

There was a lot more to the puzzle being filled in. Vasquez was the killer, but to me all four of them were guilty. The Court wasn't seeing it that way. They just hear the facts and view the evidence.

There had to be more going on behind the scenes. The world — or in this case, Binbrook — doesn't come to a screeching halt when your son is murdered. When you're a parent, everything stops.

It's like running into a brick wall. Your life has been changed forever.

You either want to kill somebody or forgive.

It was too early for forgiveness, so killing was on my mind.

I thought about Brock every minute of the day. You can't help it. If you find yourself laughing, you suddenly stop. You're not supposed to laugh when your son has been stabbed to death. You want them all to suffer the way that you are. You want their parents to feel the deep grieving loss that you're experiencing.

"F--- them all!!"

Kunic and Gashi would make the same bail as Khath. The judge certainly wasn't sympathizing with our side. There seemed to be no human element to it at all. Facts and evidence.

I was trying to fall back on my leadership skills as a player to help guide us, but when your only child has been murdered, that all flies out the window until you can catch your breath again.

When Kim came home, she phoned me via video FaceBook messenger. She had to see me to understand what I was saying.

I asked her, "Kim, did you understand what Gashi said about Vasquez? The part where Vasquez says, 'I got him, I got him real good!!'"

She started crying. It was hard enough for her, being hearing-impaired, but she was a wildcat and would have gone crazy. We both felt the same way, as did John.

Kim would get a transcript of the hearing the next day, so was able to read every word that was said. It was better for her to read it at home, because if she would have heard it in court all hell would have broken loose.

What was justice going to be for our son? This is where I was back in the prison of trauma as I call it. You're there every day and keep hearing the words of Vasquez — "I got him, I got him real good!" You don't hear the birds singing anymore. The sun doesn't shine even when it's out. Children laughing as they play together goes unheard. You're in prison!

To Plead or Not to Plead

March, 2021

It was early after the Gashi, Kunic hearing that the Crown representative contacted us and said they had been talking with Thomas Vasquez's lawyer and a plea deal was on the table: Vasquez would take responsibility for Brock's death for a reduced charge of Manslaughter, down from Murder Two, which in this case carried a five-to-seven-year sentence.

The Crown went on to say that they had very little evidence in the case, except for some DNA on the golf club that Brock struck Cam Khath with.

I agreed with the plea deal, because at least we get one of them. If we go to trial with Vasquez, maybe we lose and don't get anyone. The way the bail hearings had gone made me feel this way.

Kim and John did not agree with the plea deal. They both wanted to go to trial. We told the crown we needed some time to discuss the deal.

We now knew more facts about the case, but there was little evidence.

There was no video except of a white car. We didn't know what the police were able to do with this, but the Crown didn't think too much about it.

There were no witnesses. Everyone was inside the house at the party and the music was loud. The neighbors were used to the noise so after a while just looked away most times.

There was no murder weapon found, so Vasquez had enough time to stash it or throw it away somewhere.

The two cars established contact around 1:20 am Sunday morning. It was reported that my son and Walters decided to drive and get more beer and cigarettes for the party. Why did the owner of the house allow this?

||| THE CELL |||

They could have decided to leave on their own, but someone would have noticed them being gone so they must have agreed upon it. Brock could have said "I'll go!"

We don't know who initiated the contact on Highway 57 between the two cars, but we do know the Vasquez vehicle followed my son's car back to the house party only two blocks away.

Brock pulled up into the long driveway while Vasquez pulled in behind them tightly so they could not move.

From here, things happened quickly.

Kunic and Gashi exploded out of the car to attack Timmy Walters on the passenger side, with Kunic knocking Walters unconscious.

Brock had time to open his trunk and pull out a golf club with no head on it to fend off the oncoming attack of Cam Khath and Thomas Vasquez.

Brock was able to hit Khath once, which resulted in some DNA on the club.

From there, Vasquez was able to stab my son twice, with Gashi hearing him say, "I got him, I got him real good!" as reported at the bail hearing before they all jumped back into the car and drove away as fast as they could.

When Vasquez stabbed my son, he severed a major artery along with other internal injuries.

My son's blood was all along the driver's side of the car.

We know this, because when the car was impounded, Kim's boyfriend John knew the owner of the impound lot. They wiped the blood from the car after the police gave them the OK to release Brock's car back to John.

After Vasquez stabbed my son, Brock rolled along his car and made it to the front of the vehicle before dropping to the ground in a state of shock, bleeding out quickly.

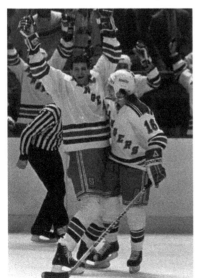

Eventually, the attendees of the house party came out and found the two of them lying on the driveway, Brock in a pool of his own blood.

Brock's girlfriend reached him first and held him while the sound of police and ambulance sirens could be heard in the distance.

The first responders tried CPR, but Brock was already gone.

They drove him to the hospital, where Kim and John had to come and identify his body. It was devastation in its lowest form: A mother had to identify her only child, body torn apart, and his stepfather of 14 years to hold her.

I could hear their cries all the way to Hong Kong.

An American Hero

March 4, 2021

Pav had been calling me lots now that he was at *The Nest*. He had the use of his phone back, so we could correspond frequently. He worried about me and told me not to do anything.

"Let the police handle it, Bubba. They will find them!" he said.

It felt good to hear his voice, and his support meant everything to me.

I was still working at my own pace and waiting, like Kim and John, for any kind of news.

Jean, Mark's sister, called me and told me she talked with Mark and he wanted to try and Zoom with the three of us.

I was excited, but neither Mark nor I were very Zoom-savvy — although I had been doing overseas calls with the court and Kim and John. That part was fairly straightforward.

I think it was scheduled for the morning, which was early evening for Jean and Pav. This was on March 1, 2021.

Once we got connected, we all laughed that Jean was the only one who knew how to do the Zoom call.

It was great to see Pav. We talked about *The Ranch,* and how it would become a reality and that we could ride horses there. He could fish and have his dog with him, just like at *The Nest*. He looked good, but I could tell this past year had taken its toll on him. We both weren't getting any younger, but *The Ranch* gave us hope.

Near the end of the call, I noticed his tone became different. I could hear it, and I could feel it. I didn't say anything. I was just so happy to see him.

We wished each other the best, said our goodbyes along with Jean, and agreed to talk soon. It was great to see Pav after so long and I felt renewed strength.

I told Kim and John, along with some friends, and they also were elated to know that I'd had a chance to see Mark. It was a shot of adrenaline that I needed to continue on.

It was late at night on March 4 when the phone rang. I wouldn't have answered it, but I saw it was Clint Malarchuk calling.

"Hi Clint, how are you doing?" I asked.

"Bubba, Mark is gone," he said.

That same heavy feeling came over me that I had when my brother Chris called to tell me about Brock's murder.

I asked, "What happened? What do you mean he's gone?"

"He committed suicide at *The Nest*."

I didn't ask any more questions. I just told Clint I had to go.

It was like being hit with a sledgehammer.

Pav was in a good place at *The Nest* with Melony Butler. How could have this happened?

I called Jean and we cried.

We talked about her mother briefly, but it was too painful to talk at any length. I think I cried all night and the next day.

Mark was now gone, along with Brock. These were two heavy blows.

Left hook to the body followed by a right uppercut!

I found out a few days later that Mark was facing a court appearance for his assault charge on Jim Miller, and it was possible he would be facing jail time.

When Jean told me this, I knew Pav wasn't going to go to any jail.

He'd already been through too much and was sick.

He told me he wasn't going to jail when he was in the psychiatric facility in St. Peter. He told me that he had a plan, and I knew what he was talking about: He would choose suicide over going to jail.

I tried to talk to him about it, but he didn't want any part of it. He was still recovering at *The Nest*.

Mark was a fragile, gentle soul. Respected, and now lost. So was I.

Wanna-Be Gangsters

After long discussions, John, Kim and I agreed with the plea deal.

Marie, our confidante in New York, also agreed. We couldn't take the chance of a trial, as all the rulings so far leaned towards the accused. To have all four get off Scot-free would have been a travesty. At least we get one.

Thomas Vasquez.

Now there was info being leaked every day, especially on Khath, Gashi, Kunic and Vasquez: They hung around together and intimidated those around them. Vasquez was the oldest and the leader. They had many friends with the same mentality. They were all big guys and threatened those around them. Was it the culture? 'I'm untouchable so I don't respect any authority'?

Nobody can touch the gangster. We all know the gangster gets killed in real life the same way I wanted Vasquez killed for taking my son's life. My faith only did so much for me. Those words by Vasquez, "I got him, I got him good!" kept playing in my head.

These guys had their way with whatever they wanted to do. The parents let them and didn't try to stop it. The Wannabe Gangster had taken over the culture, but these four had taken it to the edge.

We found out through some different groups and private citizens that told us Vasquez, Gashi, Kunic and Khath had gone to the same high schools in Binbrook as Brock at different times, so they must have known each other. We thought about this in the beginning, but you keep going around in circles.

There were two high schools in the area: Saltfleet and Sherwood.

Students could have easily overlapped.

Marie had worked her way into a couple of different Binbrook FaceBook groups and was able to view some yearbook photos and confirm this.

The police had done their interviews and they seemed to place all their efforts on catching the killer. That's what their job was: Get the killer! They had done that even with all the restrictions placed on them. They had told us at the first meeting to "Trust us," and I said, "I'll trust you." And they came through.

These four thought they were tough guys and wanted to act it out. I wish I would have been there. That guilt you carry with you so you have to shed it, as it weighs you down and drains you. It's only one phase of your early recovery but it's a step in the right direction. You accept a certain amount of responsibility as a parent.

Brock was drinking and acting irresponsible at the time before jumping in the car with Timmy Walters to go and get more beer. This doesn't mean his body should have been torn apart by a knife from Thomas Vasquez, but attending this house party and his earlier actions ultimately led him down the road to his death.

It could have easily been so different, and Brock would still be alive!

I think, when Brock came home from University, that he thought it was summer and time to party. He knew he was going back to University to study again, so he only had a certain amount of time. Brock was a man now and slightly older than his friends, except for his girlfriend, who was a year older. Her only involvement was that of being Brock's girlfriend, confirmed by triple interviews of her by police.

I thought, "Did Brock finally get to feel love from a woman during his short time at home?" I think he did, and I took solace in that.

It took some time before the sentencing for Thomas Vasquez. All the interruptions by COVID didn't stop our determination for the maximum sentence of seven years. He could, with time served, only be given the minimum sentence of five years. This could go down to three and a half years with time served. The way the courts had been making their earlier decisions, this was the stark reality.

There was first an appearance by Vasquez to set the sentencing, then the sentencing day itself. It was set for September but was delayed until October. I would follow it on Zoom.

At the beginning of the sentencing, both the defense and the Crown entered their submissions. This was where each side states its position.

The judge is the only one who makes the decision. Early on, she kept intervening and mentioned how COVID played a role in the death of my son. This was good for the defense.

I understood how COVID had affected society, especially in the Hamilton area. In 2020, Hamilton set a record for murders, with my son the 10th one.

In the summer of 2018, Brock and I had a great trip out to Vancouver.

We spent time with Big R and his family and had a chance to enjoy the beautiful Vancouver area.

We then drove the four hours to see my mother in Osoyoos.

Langley was a 30-minute drive from Vancouver, so we stopped quickly to say hello to my brother Murray and his wife Holly. Their kids, Colton and Shelby, were always active, so were only around at dinner time.

We would spend three days with them on the way back. Brock was like a brother to Colton and Shelby, and Colton — who played for the Iowa Wild, Minnesota's affiliate team — was always trying to be big brother to Brock. Shelby was a big sister.

I had asked Brock to take a year off school and come to Hong Kong with me. He was excited and agreed to it. It was May, so I told him that September would be a great time to come.

By August, I could hear rumblings in Kim's voice that Brock would not be coming. His grandmother had found a spot for him at the university in Yarmouth, where he could study mental health and recovery.

I couldn't really say no to that, but was disappointed that Brock would not be coming to Hong Kong. I wanted that year to be a special one for us.

Hong Kong was alive then. It would have been a big impact on him.

I didn't have much say in the decision and felt I lost a piece of him.

The sentencing took around four hours and was exhausting. In the end, the judge ruled that Vasquez would do the very minimum of three and a half years.

We were outraged. This is what the Crown had told us could happen, but it felt so wrong: Our son's life was worth only three and a half years. It was a tragedy, and we were living it and are going to be living it for the rest of our lives.

The reason we were able to get Vasquez was because there was an informant who came forward early in the investigation. This was the 'direction' the police kept telling us about.

The informant had first-hand recollection of Brock's killing. It took time for police to work the informant for the information needed to make the arrests.

This informant was very brave and ended up receiving the reward money. We had stated that there had to be information given to police that led to an arrest and conviction, and that criterion was met. If not for the informant, there likely would have been no arrests at all.

It was over, as far as the police were concerned. They would move on to new cases. For us, it would never be over. We would have to find ways to heal and laugh again.

For Kim, it was the hardest. Her only boy was gone. For her, the prison of trauma was a lifetime sentence. She wanted to stay in her safe little world that she had found. I never stopped loving her, even when we were apart.

There was no jealousy between John and me. John was always by her side. He was her strength now that Brock was gone. He was remarkable, really, and I loved him.

A few days after the Vasquez sentencing, Kim, John, Marie and I discussed what kind of legacy we wanted for Brock. It was only natural that we would include Pav in any decisions we thought we were going to make. This we would consult Jean on and include her in our conversations.

The Ranch identity had already been established on behalf of Mark. It was a great group of committed people led by Jean, Clint Malarchuk, Tom Gorence and Elise Rosenberg Starr. The president now was Jean and Mark's cousin Jack, an ex-military man with a cool head on his shoulders.

This we would consult Jean on and include her in our conversations.

In the early stages of *The Ranch* development, Oriana Marie and Wanda LaRusso (Wanda being the mother and Oriana Marie the daughter) were a force in the decision-making process of *The Ranch. Teammates For Life* was added and fit perfectly.

For Brock and Mark, I thought of both of them as falling stars. They would shoot across the sky but always come back. Reborn and alive in my heart.

After searching I came up with the name *Fallin Stars* with help from Marie Etts. Everything seemed to be centered around mental health. Brock had been studying mental health and recovery in Nova Scotia. Mark was held in a psychiatric facility in Minnesota. My dad, David Bruce Beck, died from dementia. It went on and on with other families. *The Ranch* and *Fallin Stars* could reach and help many people suffering from the mental health stigma.

Ourselves included.

Our logo for *Fallin Stars* was done by Ken Chinn here in Hong Kong. It has a silver B for Brock and a gold M for Mark. It signifies a rebirth.

I wanted *Fallin Stars* to concentrate on the youth of Hong Kong, to initiate programs and empower people through the arts, yoga, meditation, mindfulness and well-being, nature, music and exercise.

There is a huge wall in Chinese culture that surrounds mental health. If someone in your family has any mental health issues, then the whole family has issues. It can affect your job, so most live in silence and don't come forward for help. There has to be an open platform, so people feel comfortable discussing mental health — to make it normal, because it is. The data here suggests 1-4 people suffer from a mental health issue. I don't believe that data. I think it's everyone.

Here in Hong Kong, the suicide rate for young men is nearly two percent.

There is a problem here and it needs to be addressed. Keep it in the open and let others know they can come forward. Love and compassion go a long way.

Keeping Brock and Mark's name alive was the legacy. If it was *The Ranch* or *Fallin Stars* they would not be forgotten.

In July of 2021, when I wasn't rehired, it was my first time not working for the company in 14 years. My life was in disarray. I wasn't at the rink with the kids, and there was no office to go to. In the office, at least I had relationships with the administrators and other coaches. That was all gone now. I didn't want to leave the country after 14 years. It would be like running away from something. That would have been too easy and disrespectful.

I am the founder of *Fallin Stars,* so that means I'm the one who is financially responsible. It's not sustainable if we don't receive donations or our small line of apparel doesn't sell.

I wanted to dig in here and develop worthy partners who could help — not only with sustainability, but to develop the scholarship program on behalf of Brock and Mark. The scholarship program would benefit post-secondary students to attend local universities involving mental health and recovery, then be able to give back to the community.

This is what Brock and Mark would have wanted: A legacy that would help people.

Mark wanted a Ranch, and in the USA, it's already becoming a reality. In Hong Kong, it could be a retreat.

I always think of Brock and Mark together, so that's the brand I wanted to build with Jean's consent. They were like two rivers that slowly flowed into one. If you want to start a brand, you had better have a founder with deep pockets or a sponsor that steps in and loves what you're doing.

We have a small group with *Fallin Stars* but are determined to make inroads in the Hong Kong mental health community. Our group consists of Ady Liu and Mike Lam, then we added Marie Etts, who is our social media queen. Renee Yau also joined the group. Now Dorn Browne has been a great asset and full of energy. Brian Cheung has also helped out with his video and photo expertise.

We have been able to work with great local community partners and they have been nothing but supportive of our vision.

It's all about making mental health fun and creative. We want our philosophy to be uplifting like our website.

For myself, I am still recovering. It wasn't "Why Me?" but "What for?" That, for me, is "To Serve." To help others. Losing Brock, then Mark, has been difficult. You have to move forward, or you'll stay in the prison of trauma. Make trauma your friend and escape the prison. I do know I loved Brock more than I hate Thomas Vasquez.

Life is too short, so be kind to yourself, have fulfilling relationships and be compassionate. Hate, you have to bury —and hope it doesn't wake up.

Love conquers all.

HELPING OTHERS HEAL

Serendipity

Certain days in a person's life will be remembered always. We all go through the same customary milestones, however, every once in a while, there are truly special moments that are treasured. For Barry, I'm sure he would say it's his first NHL game, the first game as a Ranger at Madison Square Garden — and most definitely when his son, Brock, was born. I was also blessed to experience such a miraculous moment when my son, Thomas, was born. His birthday is June 14th, a day treasured by ALL New York Rangers fans after 1994, the anniversary of the team winning the Stanley Cup. My father, being a longtime Rangers' fan who carried the tradition to my brothers and me, was so proud.

After reading a draft of this book, my initial reaction was, of course, "What a roller coaster of emotions." Then, I couldn't help but realize that I was there in many of those stories — not directly, but behind the scenes, so to speak. As a fan, I could remember every hockey injury Barry received, every milestone he achieved and every disappointment and roadblock he faced. It's his story, but alongside that, there's a story of a special friendship between him and me for the last 38 years.

After seeing Barry play his first Rangers game in 1979, I felt a connection that I couldn't put into words. Can't even explain it to this day. Whatever you want to call it — "starstruck," a "crush," my mom would say, it's "puppy love."

Even as everyone around me would roll their eyes at the mention of my sentiment towards Barry, I knew he meant something to me. Whatever it was, I had it. I would constantly talk about him, watch every game and create a scrapbook of any news articles and pictures about him on and off the ice, not so secretly dreaming of a day when I would have an opportunity to meet him.

That amazing day came in August, 1984, with a chance meeting in Manhattan. My older brother had been to a party and was told Barry lived in the area, but we didn't know which building was his. So, one day, my dad drove us to the street and parked the car.

Thinking he was being funny, he said "Okay, Marie, go find Barry!" I said, "What do you mean?" He said, "Barry lives in one of these buildings. Go find him!"

THE CELL

Just as soon as he finished his sentence, Barry drove right past us in his VW Rabbit. I recognized his car from one of the Rangers' practices that we attended — and, well, I would recognize him anywhere.

We walked up to Barry and my dad introduced us. He was so polite and kind while he and my father spoke about hockey. This was the moment I had waited for, and what was I doing? Hiding behind my dad. Barry was smiling at me while the two guys spoke.

We took a few pictures and Barry walked home. Not letting this opportunity pass me by, I took note of which building was his. I began to write and send gifts to him at least a few times a month. I never received a reply, and I blamed myself for not talking to him when we first met.

The following year, I went to a Gimbles department store autograph signing in NYC. I promised myself I would speak this time. As soon as it was my turn to be at the table where he was sitting, I was ready to speak and he looked at me and said, "Hi Marie. How are you?" and got up to greet me with a hug and kiss.

I was utterly shocked that he recognized me and I had a huge smile on my face. I almost retreated again, but found a way to have a conversation.

Barry mentioned my letters and how much he liked to read them. He said they encouraged him on nights after a tough game and thought it was very nice of me to think of him. Man, if he only knew. He asked if I could keep writing, even though his schedule didn't allow time to write back. I said "Of course I will." I was glad I had the chance to thank Barry for the time he took to talk to us. He was always a fan favorite because of how he treats everyone with kindness and respect.

Barry and I continued to stay in touch. It was becoming clearer that a dream was becoming a reality. I went from being his No. 1 fan, trying to get to know him, to being close friends with him. Barry would call occasionally throughout the years; he even gave me a present for my 16th birthday with a call and a visit. He was recovering from shoulder surgery at that time, so his thoughtfulness and kindness was even more appreciated. Although it was a very difficult and uncertain time in his career, our meeting and growing friendship was a bright spot.

Serendipity is defined as a beneficial outcome that emerges from one or more chance events. We would sometimes see each other at games and hockey events until he retired and moved back to Canada and then subsequently to Hong Kong. Once computers, e-mails and Facebook happened, staying in touch became easier — even though we were oceans apart. It didn't matter which part of the world he was living in or what other relationships we've both had, Barry and I stayed connected and remained close friends. We saw each other when he came back to the US a few times also. I met his son and he met mine. It was truly a surreal and beautiful moment.

Barry and I share many mutual friends now — one special friend, in particular, is Debbie "the Hoc" Rockower. She was the president of the Rangers Fan Club in the 70's

Serendipity

and throughout the time Barry spent in New York in the 80's. Hoc and I met on Barry's Facebook and felt we had known each other forever — especially with Barry as the common link.

Barry and Hoc were very good friends, and they shared many great experiences with former teammates and The Fan Club. She was with me when we both met Brock for the first time in Connecticut, during a summer hockey camp. I saw a lot of Barry in him, and Brock thought it was cool when I pointed out that he was the same age as I was when I met his dad. They are precious memories and looking back, I'm so thankful we had that chance to spend time with Barry and Brock.

When I found out Barry's son had been murdered, I was upset down to my core — not only because of my connection to Barry, but because Brock was special to me, too, and through Barry's updates and photos I saw him grow into a caring young man. As a mom, my heart hurt for his parents, as my son was only a few years younger.

I reached out to Barry and then Kim. When Barry and I spoke via video chat, I heard the pain in his voice, I saw his eyes … he was broken-hearted. And though I felt his pain, I didn't have the right words and I was helpless. I needed to do something for him, so I offered to help Barry and Kim to set up a *GoFundMe* page for a reward. It would help capture and convict the cowards who fatally attacked Brock. It was successful and an arrest was made.

Shortly after, Barry lost his good friend and teammate Mark Pavelich and we agreed we needed to make something good come out of these tragedies. We worked well together, so Barry asked me to help him create a legacy for Brock and Mark, as well as help people in his community.

Barry wanted a mental health website and group, but not like any other site or group. He wanted to focus on positive ways to manage mental health and help people, especially those dealing with trauma — to show people how to find something good in a difficult or uncertain situation. When someone has been devastated and struggling to even pick themselves up every day, yet finds the strength and a reason to get up, that's heroic, courageous. That's Barry. He cares more about people and their needs than his own.

As a team, we organized and built it all together; came up with ideas, planned events in Hong Kong, created a meaningful and stylish logo and he bought apparel for an online store. Working together with a few of Barry's colleagues and friends in Hong Kong, we wrote and designed our website. It's called *FallinStars.org*, and it was created to be a positive place to visit, to get people talking about mental health and come up with creative ways to manage one's mental wellness. It will also host his podcast where Barry will talk about living with trauma and healing from the pain.

We also created *The Brock and Mark Scholarship Fund* for students entering college studying mental health and recovery, and the *BrockandMark.com* store, which raises mental health awareness and showcases items from the brand BROCKANDMARK. Our Launch Collection, which is still available, sold very well and we look forward to adding more merchandise in the future.

We have accomplished so much already, and I pray we continue to shine in the darkest of times. I often say to Barry "This is just the beginning." We don't always know the plan and journey in life, but we definitely get to choose who we bring for the ride. If there's one lesson that we've all been taught recently, it's to appreciate and love the people in our lives now, because there will be a day when we won't get that chance again.

Thanks, B, for choosing me — or did I choose you? Anyway, thank you for letting me be a part of your story, as you are a part of mine.

Love you.
Marie Etts Brock

||| Serendipity |||

This book is dedicated to the legacies of Brock Beck and Mark Pavelich.

Thank you to these people for being instrumental in my failures, successes and survival.

Family
Shirley Helen Beck and David Bruce Beck
Chris Beck and Family
Murray Beck and Family
Colton Beck and Family
Devon Beck and Family
Jessica Beck and Family
Wilson and Lynn Beck
Shelby Beck and Family
Jim Pike and Family
Kim Rourke
John Bialit

Close Friends of Family
Ron Greschner
JoanieTeresa Koch-Kalanj
Mike Kalanj
Denise McKenny
Donny McKenny
Brian McKenny
Rinaldo Ferrato and Family
Marie and Thomas Etts
Jean Pavelich Gevik
Trish and Angelo Lucarino
Debbie Wilson and Family
Glenn Wilson
Marcie and Mitch Ponak
Dino Rosa
Ron Petriska
Dan Huclack
Rob Ingraham and Family

Randy Shantz and Family
Mrs Hazel and Mr Don Shantz
Laura & Walter Passaglia
Karen & Ken Sieben
Wayne Pendergraft and Family
Donna Rourke and Jack Berry
Stan Smyl
Danny Clark and Mark Lofthouse
Cindy & Jim Liebel

Friends
Al Redekopp
Steve Dewell
Kyle Simms
Chris Crouzillot
John R Laroche
Gary Lawrence
Bruce Hicks
Bruce Cosford
Mark Uhrynuk
Kelly North
Jim North
Brent Worrall
Blaine Davies
Ryan Phillips
Cielo English
Dan Terrian
Rob Terrian
Dave Hudson
Randy Pierce
Mike Lam

Stu Grazier
Paul Gardner
Gigi Chow
Mike Raytek
Jethro Ludbag
Greg Smyth
Shane Weir
Valmore James
Cici Leung
Randy Pierce
Chawla Vaibhav
Anne and Freddie Delgiglio
Frank Chazen
Gus Popadopolous
Davy Curran
Julian Fla
Dr. Ash C. Moncure
David "LeRoy" Williams
Alex Sanz
Czarina Blanco
Vincent "The N!onk" G De Laura
Debbie "Hoc" Rockower
Martin Allender
Ricky & Trudy Pietsch

Teams
P.N.E. Minor Hockey Association and Members
Randy Shantz

Vancouver Junior Canucks and Members
Ron Matthews

Langley Lords and members
Gill Lundihn
Ron Livingston
Hal Yonkers

New Westminster Bruins and Members
Larry Dean
Tom Fischer
Ernie "Punch" McClean
Doug Sauter
Bill Schinske

Colorado Rockies and Members
Pat Kelly
Don Cherry
Aldo Guidolin
Tobey Wilson
Bo Webster

New York Rangers and Members
Fred Shero
Herb Brooks
Craig Patrick
Glen Sather

Los Angeles Kings and Members
Pete Demers
Bruce McNall

Vegas Golden Knights and members
George McPhee

East End Rockets and members

B.C. Lions

Hong Kong Academy of Ice Hockey
Thomas Wu
Alex Choi
Cecilia Hon
Stanley Shum
Coaches & Staff

Heroes
John Ferguson
Dick Butkus
Bobby Orr
Gordie Howe
Bobby Hull

Great Competitors
Wayne Gretzky
Mario Lemieux
Pierre Larouche
Ron Greschner
Archie Henderson
Randy Holt
Tom Laidlaw
Dave & Don Maloney
Nick Fotiu
Larry Melnyk
Andre Dore
Dave Semenko
Mark Messier
Tom Gorence
Clint Malarchuk
Reijo Ruotsalainen
Ron Delorme

Harold Snepsts
Jack McIlhargey
Clark Gillies
Bryan Trottier
Mike Bossy
Denis Potvin
Billy Smith
Danny Gare

Coaches
Scotty Bowman
Al Arbour
Herb Brooks
Don Cherry

Partners
The Ranch TFL
FallinStars.org

Printed in the USA
CPSIA information can be obtained
at www.ICGtesting.com
LVHW061353040624
782221LV00013B/92